84140

How to Win
ROTC
Scholarships

AN IN-DEPTH,
BEHIND-THE-SCENES LOOK
AT THE ROTC SCHOLARSHIP
SELECTION PROCESS

Chuck Brewer

LOST
COAST
PRESS
Fort Bragg
California

How to Win ROTC Scholarships:
An in-depth, behind-the-scenes look at the
ROTC scholarship selection process
Copyright © 2000 by C.W. Brewer
Cover design by Nancy Angelopoulos

For information, or to order additional copies, please contact:
Lost Coast Press
155 Cypress Street
Fort Bragg, California 95437
(707) 964-9520   Fax:(707) 964-7531
http://www.cypresshouse.com

Library of Congress Cataloging-in Publication Data
Brewer, C. W., 1971-
   How to Win ROTC Scholarships: An in-depth, behind the scenes look at the ROTC scholarship selection process / C.W. Brewer
      p. cm.
   ISBN 1-882-897-47-1

   1. United States. Army. Reserve Officers' Training Corps 2. United States. Air Force ROTC. 3. United States. Naval Reserve Officers Training Corps. 4. Scholarships--United States. 5. Military art and science--Scholarships, fellowships, etc. 6. Naval art and science--Scholarships, fellowships, etc. I. Title

U428.5 .B74 2000
355.2'232'71173--dc21

                                                        99-58458

Book production by Cypress House
Printed in Canada
2   4   6   8   9   7   5   3   1
First edition

DEDICATION

TO AMERICA'S VETERANS,
THANK YOU FOR YOUR SACRIFICES.
THIS COUNTRY WILL ALWAYS BE GRATEFUL.

CONTENTS

PROLOGUE

Every year, tens of thousands of high school seniors apply for ROTC scholarships. They spend hours preparing applications and writing essays in the hope of being awarded one of this country's most coveted scholarships. Totaling over eighty thousand dollars, ROTC scholarships are considered not only by students but by their parents as the last best hope for financing the prohibitive cost of a college education. Any high school senior can apply for the ROTC program and many do; however, only a small percentage of applicants receive scholarships. This book explains why. Reading this book, you will experience an "all access" view of the scholarship selection process. You will travel behind the locked doors of an ROTC scholarship board and learn what factors impact an application, and what the board wants to see in the individuals they select. Most importantly, you will learn how to market yourself as deserving of a scholarship. Nothing like this book exists, because the only people who know the ROTC selection process are active duty military personnel. No one else is allowed inside. Until now, these people have been too busy with collateral duties to document the selection process.

PREFACE

WHY THE U.S. MILITARY?

This book makes a critical assumption. It assumes that the reader is a potential applicant who already recognizes the fantastic opportunities and incredible benefits associated with military service. It would take a much larger book to identify all the potential advantages of service in the U.S. Armed Forces. Such a list could extend indefinitely if one were to consider the vast opportunities for experience that a young serviceman or woman is exposed to in today's military.

It's not the aim of this book to convince the reader that serving in the U.S. Military is the right step to take. That decision should be discussed extensively with local Armed Service recruiters. The reader of this book should already have a strong desire to not only serve in the U.S. Military, but to become one of its leaders. This book will show the reader how to express and effectively market this desire to the ROTC selection boards. It will also help students decide which branch of service is right for them.

People join the military for different reasons. Some people want to fly aircraft, while others want to parachute out of them. Some people want to drive tanks, while others want to operate complex computer systems. Like the people who join the military, the possibilities are also varied. However, one common factor pervades: they all want to serve their country. These young men and women are patriotic. They take considerable pride in the fact that, unlike most Americans who only talk about patriotism, their actions demonstrate theirs.

IS ROTC RIGHT FOR YOU?

Do you want: (among many other things):

- a résumé filled with accomplishments after you graduate from college?
- to develop more confidence, discipline and practical skills?
- the opportunity to sharpen your leadership skills so that virtually every employer will want you?
- to be a cut above your peers?
- the chance to fly the most technically advanced aircraft?
- opportunities for world travel?
- respect and/or appreciation from your peers and community?

If the answer is "yes" to any of these questions, then you should consider ROTC.

If you're looking for a college scholarship and find these benefits appealing, then the military is probably right for you. Military service changes people for the better. It makes them stronger, both physically and mentally. But, more importantly, it molds them into determined and self-confident leaders. Much of the above list identifies changes that take place within the individual. However, it's difficult to quantify the positive changes within a person. The best way to determine the intangible benefits of military service is to take a look at society's leaders, on both a local and a federal level. Many of these well-respected leaders have a common background of military service somewhere in their pasts. Military service can mold you into this type of leader.

Again, this book assumes that you have already decided that an ROTC scholarship would be an acceptable route. If, however, you're still unclear about the reserves program, the next chapter provides some background information. After reading this background, the next logical step is to determine which branch of the service is right for you. Once you've made this decision, we can then focus on crafting an application that will convince the military that you are right for it.

So, let's get started.

How to Win
ROTC
Scholarships

1

WHAT IS AN ROTC SCHOLARSHIP?

The term "ROTC" is one of many mysterious abbreviations that you will encounter during the application process for a military scholarship. The military's use of acronyms can be overwhelming for applicants. However, of all the military acronyms, "ROTC" is the most recognizable. Despite its widespread recognition, few people know that it stands for Reserve Officer Training Corps. ROTC, in some form or another, has existed since 1819 (Westpoint, NY). ROTC scholarship programs were started during the 1960s. This program is an enduring part of American society and the single largest source of young officers for the Armed Services. Basically, ROTC programs supply college-trained officers to the Army, Air Force, Navy, and Marine Corps. More than a thousand colleges and universities throughout the United States offer these programs.

Although the military has reduced in size, it still needs thousands of new officers each year. The ROTC program will be around for a long time and, as a result, there will continue to be scholarships to entice the best and brightest of America's youth. With the exception of the service academies, its success in producing effective military leaders is virtually unmatched.

It's important to note that not every ROTC student in America's colleges is the recipient of an ROTC scholarship. In fact, many students belong to ROTC programs without having received any major financial incentive. These students have other means of paying for college and have joined an ROTC program because they share with their peers (who are ROTC scholarship recipients) the desire to become officers in America's Armed Forces. Together, these students make up ROTC units across the country. Upon graduation, they will form a new generation of junior officers in America's military.However, this book is primarily concerned with the "ins and outs" of the application process for those students who do wish to receive an ROTC scholarship. The process is highly competitive, and in order to become one of the minority who actually wins a full scholarship, students must treat this process as carefully as they would treat an application to an Ivy League college.

NUTSHELL VIEW

The process works as follows: In some manner you develop an interest in ROTC and, potentially, in a scholarship as well. By speaking with a recruiter, or by sending in an information card (which you can find in the back of many ROTC information booklets), you will be sent a scholarship application. Normally, you will need to prove that you are qualified to apply for these scholarships. The qualifications include such issues as citizenship, grade point average (GPA), and Scholastic Aptitude Test (SAT) or American College Testing (ACT) scores. If you are qualified, or have the potential to qualify, you must finish completing the ROTC scholarship application. An interview will then be scheduled with either a recruiting officer or an ROTC admissions counselor. Note that during the time in which you are applying for an ROTC scholarship, you should also be applying for admission at the colleges or universities that have an ROTC program or an affiliation program with another campus. A selection board then reviews your application and compares your qualifications with those of other applicants. Much like the college admissions process, you will be notified of the board's decision regarding your application. If you are awarded a scholarship, you will have one to two weeks to accept or to defer the award. If you are denied the scholarship, the board will still encourage you to join an ROTC unit, because you can always reapply the next year for two or three-year scholarships.

If you accept the scholarship, you will attend one of the schools where you have been admitted. The U.S. Military will pay for your tuition, student fees, textbooks, and an allowance of one hundred and fifty dollars per month. While at school, your military education will consist of taking a predetermined number of classes in Military Science. During the summers, you will receive military training opportunities such as Airborne Jump School or a midshipman "summer cruise" on a U.S. warship. Once you graduate from college, you will receive a commission in the U.S. Armed Forces. It's at this point that your active military service begins.

RESERVE?

The word "Reserve" often confuses people. For potential ROTC applicants, it means that you will serve as an active duty officer in the U.S. Armed Forces for a period of time, after which you can expect to be a member of this country's reserve military forces. The United States military is struc-

3

tured so that it relies upon the Reserve Components (RC), the National Guard, and the active duty portions of each branch in any minor conflict. The Reserve Component's basic mission is to support the total force of the U.S. Military. They produce a reserve component force trained to mobilize, deploy, merge with the active duty units, gain command, fight, and win when called upon in times of national emergency. Thus, the units and the personnel in the Reserve Components aren't merely "forces in reserve." They are a major part of the U.S. Military's mission to preserve our country's freedom and defend our national interests.

A good example of the proportional relationship that the Reserve Components have with the active duty side of each branch is the fact that the Army Reserves and Army National Guard comprise more than half of the entire U.S. Army. More armor, mechanized infantry, field artillery, and cavalry units exist in the Reserve Component than in the active Army, and over two-thirds of the Army's combat support units belong to the Reserves. You can begin to see the major role that the Reserve personnel play in making the total forces of the U.S. military work as strongly as they do.

The Reserves can be divided into two categories: active and inactive. Active reserve units meet and train on a regular basis. The phrase "one weekend a month and two weeks during the summer" refers to this training. The reservist is usually paid for his training, and his participation counts towards military retirement points. Inactive reserves consist of service men and women who have elected not to train once a month, but who have agreed to be called to active duty should the need arise. Together, the active and inactive reservists comprise a staggering number of service personnel. The active reserve units are located all over the continental United States, and are intended to augment the active military strength in times of crisis, such as Operation Desert Storm.

The key to understanding ROTC scholarships is that for every year of college that ROTC finances, you agree to serve twelve to eighteen months of active duty in return. Is there a standard contract length? Yes. Generally, four years of college equals four to six years of active service. This deal is not bad if you consider that you'll have no college loans and a well-paid, full-time job when you graduate. Add to that the incredible experiences you'll have during your tour of active duty, and it's no wonder this scholarship is so highly desired.

Furthermore, consider that (1) yearly tuition at an average, private college costs at or over twenty thousand dollars, and (2) student fees and textbooks can amount to up to five thousand dollars per year. Potentially, an ROTC scholarship can be valued at roughly one hundred and twenty thousand dollars during a four-year period. Of course, it all depends on the costs associated with your particular college or university and the type of ROTC scholarship that you're awarded, but the ROTC program is by far the best deal around. The military will pay up to twenty thousand dollars per year for your tuition. As mentioned above, the military will also pay the additional costs of your education, such as student fees and textbook costs. And, as if these benefits weren't enough, the ROTC program will pay you a monthly allowance of one hundred and fifty dollars to ensure that you spend time on your studies rather than at a part-time job. Given free tuition, fees, and books, along with a monthly allowance? You can see why ROTC scholarships are so popular. Few scholarships in the United States are this comprehensive.

GENERAL ELIGIBILITY REQUIREMENTS

As with almost every scholarship, applicants must meet pre-determined requirements for eligibility. Because the Federal Government offers the scholarships, the requirements of ROTC scholarship programs are extremely fair. They cannot and will not discriminate on factors such as gender, race, or income. The ROTC selection board will grant or deny you a scholarship based solely on your qualifications. However, due to the nature of this program, it is reasonable to expect certain eligibility requirements. Although individual service requirements are listed in Chapter Two, below are some requirements common to most ROTC programs.

• You must be a United States citizen.

• You must be seventeen years of age by October of your senior year, and not be over twenty-seven years of age by the time you graduate college and receive your commission. Prior military service would make you eligible for a waiver and for a possible extension of the age requirement. An one-year extension is granted for every year of military service. The maximum extension is three years.

• You must be a high school graduate or hold an equivalent certificate/diploma the following year after you apply.

• You cannot have any personal convictions that would prevent you from supporting and defending the Constitution of the United States or conscientiously bearing arms.

• An explanation must be provided for any arrest and/or civil conviction.

• You must meet GPA and SAT/ACT requirements set by the given service.

OBLIGATIONS

There is no such thing as a free lunch. While that saying is a cliché, most applicants don't realize that accepting an ROTC scholarship means committing to active duty and reserve service. It is not uncommon for ROTC scholarship students to finish four years of an all-expenses paid education and then decide that they don't want to be in the military. However, breaking your contract with the Unites States Government has serious repercussions. If you decide to not fulfill your end of the bargain, you must repay the money you've spent (this situation will be covered in-depth later). When you accept the scholarship, understand that you must fulfill certain obligations. Some common obligations are:

Sign a contractual obligation with the given service

This contract contains the terms of your agreement. As mentioned before, most of the services have similar terms in their contracts. For example, the military offers you an ROTC scholarship, and in return you agree to serve six years of active service as well as some reserve service (keep in mind that the terms of this agreement have been known to vary as the manpower needs of the Armed Forces change). There will be a clause within this contract, stating that you agree to reimburse all scholarship money if you break the terms of the signed contract. The Government can ask for its money back or it can make you enlist in a particular branch of service. The choice belongs entirely to them. You should understand this contract before your senior year in college brings a change of heart. Don't break the contract.

Maintain studies in a chosen curriculum

If, for example, you have indicated some field of engineering or nursing as your ROTC program, you must attend an accredited school with that field of study in its curriculum. For example, the military carefully selects nursing applicants based on manpower projections of its services. They are reluctant to allow ROTC students the latitude of switching studies.

Attend an advanced training camp between your junior and senior year

As stated before, the advanced training camp can range from Airborne Jump School to a four-week, midshipman "summer cruise" on a U.S. naval warship. Every service branch sponsors different advanced camps to familiarize their students with the important aspects of that particular branch.

Obligate yourself to the Reserves (active or inactive) for a period of up to eight years

Joining the Reserves is truly the main purpose of an ROTC student so participation in the active or inactive reserves is expected.

Accept a commission to serve on active or Reserve duty upon finishing your collegiate degree

This chapter offered an overview of the application process, which will be examined in-depth later. This overview, through its description of the Reserves, attempted to help you better understand what it means to apply for an ROTC scholarship. With that understanding, one can begin to look at the types of services, eligibility criteria, and potential obligations in order to establish who can apply. The military sets these criteria for good reasons and, when it comes to standards, they usually remain inflexible. If you don't meet the eligibility requirements, you should stop reading this book and focus on how you can become eligible. For example, if retaking the SAT/ACTs, or improving your high school GPA will make you eligible, then get started immediately.

The next chapter is geared towards selecting the branch of service that interests you, and then finding the appropriate program within the branch. Although most applicants enter the application process with tendencies towards one branch or another, these preferences usually have to do with familiarity, family history, and personal goals. One chapter cannot adequately depict all the advantages, elements, and nuances of each of the four branches. With that said, the best resource for finding more information on the various branches is local Armed Forces recruiters. It's their job to educate people about the advantages of their particular services, and they will be happy to speak with you. (See Appendix A for the phone numbers of the four branches.)

2

WHICH SERVICE IS RIGHT FOR YOU?

This chapter is designed to give you a broad overview of the four branches, in addition to specifics about each of their ROTC programs. Hopefully, by reading this overview, you will begin to recognize which service best suits your interests. With this new understanding, it's your responsibility to contact your local ROTC recruiter and further investigate a specific service.

Some applicants choose a particular service based on the colleges that they want to attend. Others select their service based on specific interests such as aviation, science, or communications. Whatever the reason, there is no wrong reason to choose a service, provided that it's what you want and not what somebody else wants. Remember that choosing a branch of the military is your decision and one that you will have to live with for a lifetime. Make sure that you act with your own interests in mind. While some branches have occupations unique to them, applicants considering any branch of service will find that almost every career opportunity is available. With that said, the determinant in choosing a service should come from the desire to be a part of one particular service.

U.S. NAVY/MARINE OPTION ROTC

The Naval Reserve Officers Training Corps (NROTC) Program was established in 1926 to educate a broad base of citizens in the arts and sciences of Naval Warfare. The program provided an opportunity for young men to undertake careers in the naval profession. As a result of its success, the program quickly evolved. In the beginning, there were six NROTC units located at the University of California at Berkeley, Georgia Institute of Technology, Northwestern University, University of Washington, Harvard University, and Yale University. In June of 1930, one hundred and twenty-six midshipmen graduated from college and received commissions in the United States Navy.

The Marine Corps entered the NROTC Program in 1932, offering commissions in the United States Marine Corps to qualified NROTC graduates. In 1968, Prairie View A&M became the first Historically Black College (HBC) to host the program. In 1972, the Secretary of the Navy allowed sixteen women to enroll in the program and to attend school at any one of four colleges. Women may now participate in the program while attending any NROTC affiliated college or university.

SPECIFICS ABOUT TODAY'S PROGRAM

The mission of today's NROTC Program is to develop young men and women morally, mentally, and physically, and to instill in them the highest ideals of duty, honor, and loyalty. The program educates and trains young men and women for leadership and management positions in an increasingly technical Navy and Marine Corps. There are currently fifty-seven NROTC units, located at sixty-nine sites throughout the United States. Over one hundred colleges and universities host NROTC units or have cross-enrollment agreements with a host university. The Navy's annual goal for ROTC commissions is 1050, while the Marine Corps' goal is 225 (i.e., the Navy and Marine Corps hope to have, respectively, 1050 and 225 ROTC midshipmen graduate from college every year). Selected applicants for the program are awarded scholarships through a highly competitive national selection process and recipients receive full tuition, books, fees and other financial benefits at many of the country's leading colleges and universities. Upon graduation, midshipmen are commissioned as officers in the Naval or Marine Corps Reserve.

Students selected for the NROTC Scholarship Program make their own arrangements for college enrollment, including room and board, and take the normal course load required by the college or university for degree completion. Additionally, scholarship midshipmen are required to follow specific academic guidelines. These guidelines generally refer to a curriculum that meets NROTC standards.

ABOUT THE NAVY

If you like the water, you will love the Navy. You will not spend all of your time swimming, but you can expect to encounter a lot of water in any naval career. The Navy offers many of the same opportunities that each of the other services offers. It provides opportunities in aviation, engineering, nursing, communications, military intelligence, finance, and Special Forces (SEALS)—and that list only scratches the surface of the occupation specialties.

The Navy is the only service (excluding the USMC) who bears its strength at sea. The Navy's strength lies in its ability to cover the globe with a limited amount of resources and to operate at optimum efficiency. As a result, personnel that thrive in the Navy usually enjoy traveling and seeing new places. The only strange part about the traveling is that it transpires on U.S. warships and it can take months to travel from port to port.

The Navy has a vast array of ships (including submarines) at bases all over the world. These base locations range from small islands in the South Pacific to major naval bases on the United States coasts. At sea, naval aviation has its strongest presence onboard U.S. aircraft carriers. Some people liken these enormous ships to floating cities, with as many as five thousand sailors and marines on board. Regardless of the class of a naval ship, its efficiency and power is a direct result of the equipment and resources available to the servicemen on board.

ABOUT THE MARINES

Many people think of the U.S. Marine Corps as a separate branch of service. However, technically, the Marine Corps is a department of the Navy. One can explain the role of the Marine Corps by describing them as the Army of the Navy. The Marines coexist with the sailors on naval ships and tackle any ground engagements that may arise in a theater of operations. Although not every Navy ship has Marines onboard, many of the larger ships do. This role is why many people refer to the U.S. Marines as "America's 911 force." One of the rarely known facts about the Marine Corps is its size. At roughly 175,000 marines, the USMC is about twenty-percent of the size of the U.S. Army. Despite its relatively small size, the Marines carry a powerful punch and a proud tradition that dates back to its founding in 1775. Few people know that U.S. Marines serve as security guards at U.S. Embassies around the world.

By breaking down the structure of the U.S. Marine Corps,

one can see that it contains a microcosm of all the branches in the U.S. Armed Forces. The Marines have a strong aviation capability, a strong ground combat capability, and a strong naval presence, similar to the Air Force, Army, and Navy. This microcosm indicates that any occupation found in the other branches can potentially be found in the Marines, only to a smaller extent.

Although the Marines belong to the Navy, not all marines experience sea duty. Many marines, because of their vocation, are stationed at bases in or outside of the continental United States and never see the inside of a ship. The difference between the Marine Corps and the other services rests in its assigned role in the mission of the U.S. Military. The Marine Corps is the initial engagement force in any amphibious (i.e., sea to land) conflict. On a final note, the Marines have a reputation for being a tough service, both physically and mentally. While this reputation is true to some extent, every branch of service has its own challenging elements.

TYPES OF **NROTC** SCHOLARSHIPS

The following list represents the available scholarships within NROTC:
    Four-Year Scholarship Navy Option
    Four-Year Scholarship Marine Option
    Two-Year Scholarship
    Two-Year College Program
    Four-Year Navy Nurse

Four-Year Scholarship Navy Option

Selected applicants for the NROTC scholarship program earn scholarships through a competitive national selection process. Upon graduation, the recipient will be commissioned as a naval officer, committed to a minimum of four years active duty in the U.S. Navy. The scholarship recipient will receive full tuition and other financial benefits, including books, class fees and one hundred and fifty dollars per month subsistence. NROTC scholarships do not pay for room and board or personal items such as computers.

Applicants for four-year NROTC scholarships must meet these eligibility requirements:

1. You must be a United States citizen.
2. You must be at least seventeen years of age by September 1st of the year you are starting college and less than twenty-seven years of age on June 30th of the year in which you are eligible for graduation and commissioned status. An age waiver may be granted for prior active military service, on a month-to-month basis, computed as of September 1st of the year of enrollment in NROTC, provided you will not reach your thirtieth birthday by June 30th of the year in which graduation and commissioning are anticipated.
3. You must be a high school graduate or possess an equivalency certificate by August 1st of the year you are applying.
4. You must have no moral or personal convictions which prevent the bearing of arms in defense of the United States, and you must be deemed physically qualified.
5. You must meet minimum SAT test scores of 530 verbal and 520 math or a minimum composite ACT test score of 22 in both English and math. (Scores subject to change).
6. You are also responsible for gaining acceptance to a certified NROTC university. Acceptance does not guaran-

tee assignment to that school, so it is recommended that you apply to at least three of your desired universities.

Students who have more than one year of college credit are not eligible for the four-year scholarship. They should discuss other options with the professor of naval science at their university.

Four-Year Scholarship Marine Option

Application eligibility for the NROTC scholarship Marine Option program is the same as the Navy four-year EXCEPT that the minimum SAT test score is 1000 and the minimum ACT composite test score is a 45 combined score for the English and Math portions.

Two-Year Scholarship

The two-year scholarship program covers tuition, fees, textbooks, uniforms, and a one hundred and fifty dollars per month subsistence for a maximum of twenty academic months during the junior and senior years of college only. Students applying for this scholarship have already completed at least one year of college.

Two-Year College Program

The two-year college program is a non-subsidized program that covers uniforms and one hundred and fifty dollars per month subsistence for twenty academic months during the junior and senior years of college. This program is for students who wish to participate in NROTC without scholarship money.

Four-Year Navy Nurse

Four-year scholarships are available to students interested in pursuing a Bachelor of Science degree in nursing. Those selected must be accepted into a nursing program. Completion of the program leads to a commission in the Navy Nurse Corps.

FACULTY

The teaching staff of Naval ROTC units is composed of experienced, career Naval and Marine officers. Their various experiences, academic background and qualifications as instructors determine selection, and officers in the grades of captain through colonel, with five or more years remaining before retirement, are eligible. Generally, these instructors will have advanced degrees and or strong leadership qualities that prompted their selection to an ROTC instructor position.

ACTIVE DUTY SERVICE COMMITMENTS

Midshipmen selected for ROTC scholarships are contracted to accept a commission as an Ensign (Navy) or as a Second Lieutenant (Marine Corps) after completing all NROTC and academic degree requirements. Most midshipmen are obligated to a minimum of four years on active duty. However, pilots are obligated to an eight to ten year commitment after completing specialized undergraduate pilot training and navigators (co-pilots) can expect a six to eight year commitment after completing specialized undergraduate navigator training. The potential for the aviation service commitments to lengthen is very real, and could reasonably be expected.

Navy-Marine Corps ROTC
SCHOLARSHIP INFORMATION

For more information about Navy/Marine Option ROTC programs and scholarship applications, write to: NROTC Scholarship Program, Navy Recruiting Command, (Code 314), 4015 Wilson Blvd., Arlington, VA 22203-1991. See Appendix A for phone numbers and website address.

U.S. ARMY ROTC

Captain A. Partridge, a superintendent at Westpoint, established Army ROTC in 1819. He began the program with the belief that this country needed more "citizen soldiers." His program spread quickly to colleges and universities across the country. By the turn of the century, one hundred and five schools offered military instruction on their campuses. Today, there are over 1300 colleges with Army ROTC programs.

ABOUT THE U.S. ARMY

The U.S. Army is huge. It supports over a million servicemen and women on active duty, and can call upon over a million more service personnel (if one counts the U.S. Army National Guard and U.S. Army Reserves). Two million people are more than the population of many United States cities. Imagine the multitude of occupations involved in sustaining such a sizable force. The advantages of the U.S. Army are reflected in its vast array of career opportunities. Everybody knows that the U.S. Army has infantry and artillery officers, but you can also be a finance manager, an optometrist, or a computer-programming officer. The Army has every conceivable job somewhere within its structure and ROTC is the perfect way to get there.

Being such a sizable service, the Army also receives an enormous budget from the defense department. This fact might be irrelevant now, but it will directly affect your active duty experiences. Among the infantrymen, the military is notorious for having substandard equipment. However, the Army is the exception. While the other services are improving, the U.S. Army has already fielded incredibly advanced equipment to its soldiers. The Army's extensive budget allows Army personnel to attend cutting-edge military schools (e.g., airborne or survival training).

Many people are aware of the Army's capable infantry, but few people comprehend the strength behind its other occupational fields, such as aviation, armor, artillery, air defense, engineering, intelligence, communications, law, finance, and medicine. In reality, these fields are where a young officer can learn and master a job skill that will make him or her attractive to civilian employers.

SPECIFICS ABOUT TODAY'S PROGRAM

The Army ROTC four-year program provides college-trained officers for the Army, Army Reserve and Army National Guard. As the largest single source of Army officers, the ROTC program fulfills a vital role in providing mature young men and women for leadership and management positions in an increasingly technical Army.

ARMY ROTC FOUR-YEAR SCHOLARSHIP PROGRAM

Students earn U.S. Army ROTC four-year scholarships through a highly competitive national selection process. Scholarships pay up to sixteen thousand dollars a year for college tuition and education fees. A designated book allowance is an additional benefit. However, you can't apply these scholarship benefits towards room and board. Army scholarship recipients also receive a tax-free subsistence allowance of one hundred and fifty dollars a month for up to ten months for each year the scholarship is in effect. The Army does grant two and three-year ROTC scholarships. These scholarships are generally awarded to students who are already on campus. Check with the ROTC unit commander for the availability of these scholarships.

Like the other services, the U.S. Army allows scholarship students to lead the same life as other college students. Students may pursue any course of study leading to a bachelor's degree that is listed in what the Army calls the Approved Academic Disciplines List. They may engage in any activity that does not interfere with ROTC requirements, which include prescribed Military Science Courses, participation in scheduled drill periods, and attending a six-week ROTC Advanced Camp between the junior and senior years. Upon successful completion of ROTC and bachelor's degree requirements, you will be commissioned as a second lieutenant in the Active Army, Army Reserve, or the National Guard.

Traditionally, Army ROTC is a four-year program. The first two years, the freshman and sophomore years, comprise the Basic Course. Keep in mind that you can take the Basic Course on a trial basis for up to two years (unless, of course, you're on an Army ROTC scholarship). The second two years, the junior and senior years, make up the Advanced Course. The summer between your junior and senior years, you will attend the Advanced Camp.

During the Basic Course, your studies will include Basic Leadership Development, Basic Military Skills, Adventure Training, and Life Skills. During the Advance Course, your studies will include Advanced Leadership and Management Skills, Advanced Tactics, and Army Ethics.

Selection criteria

The U.S. Army sets forth the following criteria for selection of all scholarship applicants:

- Results of the SAT/ACT. You must achieve a minimum SAT composite score of 920 or an ACT composite score of 19 to qualify for competition. If both tests have been taken, the better of the two will be considered.
- High school academic standing. Your class size and rank are required.
- Three school officials' evaluations. These evaluations are to be completed by teachers, coaches, or a high school principal. If you are attending the United States Military Academy (USMA) Preparatory School, you must have one of these evaluations completed by an USMA Preparatory School Official.
- Extracurricular participation, athletic activities, and leadership positions held. If you had a part-time job during the school year and did not have the time for extensive participation in sports and extracurricular activities, you will be given credit based on the number of hours you worked per week.

U.S. Army ROTC/Nursing

Army ROTC Nursing majors compete for two, three, and four-year scholarships. Army ROTC nurse cadets combine college electives in military science and summer training experience with a regular nursing program. Upon completion of the program (and provided all prerequisites are met), you will receive a commission as an officer in the Army Nurse Corps.

Faculty

The teaching staff of Army ROTC units is often hand picked in order to ensure that the brightest and most experienced Army officers will serve as examples for AROTC cadets. Very often the vocations of these instructors have exposed them to experiences that only enhance the learning environment for cadets. Officers in the grades of captain through colonel, with five or more years remaining before retirement, are eligible. As it is with most of the other services, these instructors will have advanced degrees.

Active-Duty service commitments

Cadets selected for Army ROTC scholarships are contracted to accept a commission as a Second Lieutenant in the U.S. Army after completing all AROTC and academic degree requirements. Most cadets are obligated to a minimum of four years on active duty. However, pilots are often obligated for longer commitments due not only to the length of their schooling, but to the quality of the training they receive.

Army ROTC scholarship information

For more information about Army ROTC programs and scholarship applications, write to: Army ROTC, HQ ROTC Cadet Command, Fort Monroe, VA 23651-5238 or call 1 (800) USA ROTC. See Appendix A for phone numbers and website address.

AIR FORCE ROTC

The first Air ROTC units were established between 1920 and 1923 at the University of California at Berkeley, Georgia Institute of Technology, the University of Illinois, the University of Washington, Massachusetts Institute of Technology, and Texas Agricultural and Mechanical College (now Texas A&M University). After World War II, General Dwight D. Eisenhower, Chief of Staff of the War Department, signed General Order No. 124, establishing Air ROTC units at seventy-seven colleges and universities throughout the nation. In 1964, the ROTC Vitalization Act authorized a new two-year college level (senior) program, a high school level (junior) program, and scholarships. An experimental program to commission women through Air Force ROTC was first conducted from 1956 to 1960. Starting in 1969, women were again enrolled in the college level program, and in the high school (junior) program four years later. In addition, eligible enlisted Air Force personnel pursuing a college degree, who are interested in becoming commissioned officers, can compete in the Air Force ROTC Airman Scholarship and Commissioning Program, established in 1973. In 1978, Air Training Command, with headquarters at Randolph AFB, Texas, assumed responsibility for Air Force ROTC programs.

ABOUT THE AIR FORCE

The importance of the Air Force's aerospace mission underscores the need for flight, science, space operations, engineering, and missile officers. The complexity of modern aviation, space technology, and communications generates a critical need for top quality engineers, scientists, and computer scientists. The Air Force likes to foster these experts from the beginning; hence, the ROTC program. Officers are also needed in non-technical, general management areas. Like the Army and Navy, the Air Force is an enormous service that requires every imaginable occupation in order to keep it operating efficiently. Most of these occupations relate to ensuring the mission capable status of the Air Force. Some of these fields include intelligence, meteorology, personnel, finance, chemical engineering, nuclear engineering, mechanical engineering, civil engineering, aeronautical engineering, architectural engineering, transportation, air traffic controller, public affairs, and space and missile operations. While there are exceptions, most jobs in the Air Force pertain to aviation or operations which support it.

Specifics about today's program

Air Force Reserve Officer Training Corps' headquarters is located at Maxwell Air Force Base in Alabama. This program is the largest source of commissioned officers for the Air Force. AFROTC's mission statement reflects its goal: "to produce leaders for the Air Force and better citizens for America." Based on Air Force requirements, the AFROTC program recruits, educates, and commissions officer candidates through college-level programs. As of April 1998, ROTC units were located at one hundred and forty-three colleges and universities throughout the United States and Puerto Rico. Furthermore, there are over eight hundred cross-town enrollment programs or consortium agreements wherein students from schools near Air Force ROTC host institutions can attend classes.

PROGRAMS

Air Force ROTC offers two routes to an Air Force commission: two-year and four-year programs. Students enroll in Air Force ROTC classes at the same time and in the same manner as they would for other college courses. ROTC courses normally receive academic credit as part of a student's electives. At each host institution, ROTC is a separate academic department. Each instructor is an active duty Air Force officer with at least a master's degree, and the academic rank of assistant professor. The unit commander has an academic rank of full professor. Recent enrollments in the college programs have ranged from a high of 22,067 students in 1988 to an estimated low of 10,231 students in 1993.

Four-year program

The first two years of the Air Force ROTC four-year program, the General Military Course, consist of one hour of classroom work and one to two hours of leadership laboratory each week. Cadets who wish to compete for entry into the last two years of the program, the Professional Officer Course, must do so under the requirements of the Professional Officer Course Selection System. This system uses qualitative factors such as grade point average, unit commander evaluation, and aptitude test scores to determine a student's officer potential. After selection, students must complete a four-week, field-training encampment at an assigned Air Force base before entering the course. Cadets enrolled in the Professional Officer Course attend class three hours a week and participate in a weekly, one to two hour leadership laboratory.

In the Professional Officer Course, cadets apply what they have learned in the General Military Course and at field-training encampments. Cadets conduct the leadership laboratories and manage the unit's cadet corps. Each unit's cadet corps is based on the Air Force organizational pattern of flight, squadron, group, and wing. Professional Officer Course classes are small, with an emphasis on group discussions and cadet presentations. Classroom topics include management, communication skills, and national defense policy.Once enrolled in the Professional Officer Course, cadets are enlisted in the Air Force Reserve and assigned to a reserve section. This assignment entitles them to a monthly, nontaxable allowance of one hundred and fifty dollars during the academic year.

Two-year program

The Air Force ROTC two-year program, and the last two years of the four-year program are the same at the Professional Officer Course level. However, the entry procedures for the two programs differ. Entrance into the Professional Officer Course is highly competitive and two-year applicants must be chosen through the selection system described above. Two-year applicants must also complete a six-week field-training encampment. The additional two weeks of field-training for the two-year applicants prepare them for entry into the Professional Officer Course. Two-year applicants are not committed to the Air Force until they return to school in the fall, and make the decision to enroll in Air Force ROTC.

One-year program

The one-year ROTC program was created in order to fill shortages in certain occupational fields within the Air Force. For example, if the Air Force finds that it has a current shortage of chemical engineers (CE), it will open its one-year program specifically to undergraduates majoring in CE. Currently, undergraduate nursing and meteorological students in their junior years are eligible for the program. This program is also available to law students on a case-by-case basis. Those selected for the one-year program attend a five-week field-training encampment during the summer before entering the Professional Officer Course as contract cadets. These cadets also receive a monthly subsistence allowance of one hundred and fifty dollars during the academic year. After completing all requirements, the cadets are commissioned as Air Force officers with a four-year active duty service commitment.

Scholarships covering full tuition, books and fees are available for this program. To qualify for an one-year program scholarship, students must be younger than twenty-five years of age as of June 30th of the calendar year in which they will be commissioned. Those who do not qualify for a scholarship may still participate in the one-year program as non-scholarship cadets. However, such cadets must be younger than thirty years of age before entering active duty. Once a student is selected for the one-year program, change of academic major is not permitted, unless it is in the best interest of the Air Force.

Special programs

There are Air Force ROTC programs that provide cadets with specialized, off-campus learning experiences. In most cases, field-training is a cadet's first exposure to a working, Air Force environment. The program develops military leadership and discipline, while providing Air Force officer orientation and motivation. At the same time, the Air Force can evaluate each cadet's potential as an officer. Field-training includes aircraft and aircrew orientation, Air Force professional development orientation, marksmanship training, junior officer training, physical fitness, and survival training. Uniforms, lodging, and meals are provided at no cost to the cadet, and cadets travel at Air Force expense to and from school. Additionally, after applicable deductions, cadets receive pay of about five hundred dollars for the four-week encampment and about six hundred and twenty-five dollars for the five-week summer camp.The advanced training program provides cadets with specialized and individual professional development. The learning experience is similar to an intern program in which cadets are placed at Air Force bases to become acquainted with life, duties, and responsibilities of Air Force men and women. The advanced training program is a voluntary program that provides an important transition for a cadet between training and commissioning.

Usually, cadets are assigned to Air Force bases for two to three-week periods. They receive approximately nineteen dollars a day, meals, living quarters, and are reimbursed for travel expenses to and from the base. Limited opportunities are also available for parachuting, glider, and survival training courses. Base visits give cadets a firsthand look at operational Air Force bases. An assigned Air Force ROTC instructor adds personal knowledge of the Air Force mission to the cadets' base-visit experience. This program is beneficial to the education and training of Air Force ROTC cadets because it develops an appreciation of the Air Force professional environment.

SCHOLARSHIPS

Current emphasis in the Air Force ROTC college scholarship program is to award scholarships to candidates pursuing undergraduate engineering or other scientific and technical disciplines. Nearly ninety percent of Air Force ROTC scholarships are awarded in these disciplines. However, students in every degree program enjoy scholarship opportunities, as the Air Force wants to attract students who excel both academically and militarily.

The majority of scholarships are awarded in increments of two, three and four-year periods. Air Force ROTC offers three types of scholarships. Type I covers full tuition and most required fees. Type II covers tuition and fees up to nine thousand dollars annually—an award that covers the cost at most United States colleges and universities. Type II awards constitute the majority of awards offered via the College Scholarship Program. Targeted scholarships of the College Scholarship Program are awards designated specifically for lower cost, in-state institutions. Targeted institutions are selected based on the candidate's list of desirable schools. All awards provide funds for books, most required fees, and a monthly nontaxable subsistence allowance of one hundred and fifty dollars.

In addition, Air Force ROTC has an incentive scholarship program for cadets contracted into the Professional Officer Course. This incentive scholarship pays up to two thousand dollars annually. It is available to nearly all Professional Officer Course contracted cadets who do not receive scholarship benefits, and who are otherwise eligible for incentive entitlements.

All scholarship cadets are required to meet certain academic, military, and physical fitness standards to earn and maintain scholarship benefits. All non-prior service scholarship recipients must be younger than twenty-five years of age as of June 30th of the calendar year during which commissioning is scheduled. Prior service applicants may have the age limit extended by the total days of active-duty military service, up to a maximum of four years.

EXTRACURRICULAR ACTIVITIES

All ROTC students in every branch of service can participate in a variety of extracurricular activities, and the Air Force ROTC cadets are no different. Several units have special drill teams, color guards, and honor guards. Many students enrolled in Air Force ROTC also participate in unit-sponsored intramural sports and social functions. Cadets pursuing a commission are eligible for membership in the Arnold Air Society, a national, honorary professional and service organization established to strengthen relations between Air Force ROTC, the Air Force, the campus, and the local community.

ENROLLMENT CRITERIA

The first two years of the Air Force ROTC college program, the General Military Course, are open to all students at least fourteen years of age. Second-year scholarship cadets and all cadets entering the last two years of the college program, the Professional Officer Course, must be at least seventeen years of age. These contract cadets must meet Air Force ROTC and Department of Defense eligibility standards ranging from physical fitness to United States citizenship.

FACULTY

The teaching staff at Air Force ROTC units is composed of well-educated and experienced Air Force officers. Professional experience, academic background, and instructor qualifications determine selection. Officers in the grades of captain through colonel, with five or more years remaining before retirement, are eligible. They normally have master's degrees and are regular or career reserve officers. Officers usually complete Air University's Academic Instructor School at Maxwell AFB before reporting for their teaching assignments.

ACTIVE-DUTY SERVICE COMMITMENTS

Cadets in the Professional Officer Course, and second-year scholarship cadets, are contract cadets who agree to accept a commission as a second lieutenant in the Air Force after completing all Air Force ROTC and academic degree requirements. Most cadets are obligated to a four-year, active-duty commitment. However, pilots are obligated to an eight-year commitment after completing specialized undergraduate pilot training. Navigators can expect a six-year commitment after completing specialized undergraduate navigator training.

MEDICAL PROFESSIONS

Nursing graduates agree to accept a commission in the Air Force Nurse Corps and serve four years on active duty after successfully completing their licensing examination. Two exam failures result in a four-year assignment as an Air Force line officer. Cadet pre-medical scholarship recipients, who are accepted into medical school within one year of graduating, are sponsored in their pursuit of medical degrees.

LEGAL PROFESSIONS

Second-year law students can pursue an Air Force commission through Air Force ROTC's graduate law program. This program guarantees judge advocate duty after the student completes all Air Force ROTC, law school, and Bar requirements. After graduating from an American Bar Association-accredited law school, the student must be admitted to practice law before the highest state court of any state or before a federal court. The new lawyer is then commissioned into the Air Force at the grade determined by the laws and directives in effect at the time of call to active duty.

AIRMAN COMMISSIONING OPPORTUNITIES

Air Force ROTC has four programs in which Air Force enlisted personnel may pursue a commission. The Leaders Encouraging Airman Development Phase I, Scholarships for Outstanding Airmen to ROTC (SOAR), allows commanders to recognize outstanding and deserving airmen by nominating them for an Air Force ROTC scholarship in any field of study. The Airman Scholarship and Commissioning Program lets airmen compete for Air Force ROTC scholarships through the desired AFROTC unit. Although any major may be selected, technical and nursing applicants are usually more favorably considered. Both programs offer two to four-year scholarships and can only be awarded for completion of a bachelor's degree. Applicants must meet age requirements as prescribed by public law.The Professional Office Course Early Release Commissioning Program is available to airmen who are not eligible for a scholarship due to age, degree program, or grade point average. Individuals compete for allocations through the Air Force ROTC program that they plan to attend. These three Air Force ROTC programs require the selected airmen to leave active duty to complete their degrees and Air Force requirements necessary to earn a commission.

Junior ROTC program

Although participation in the Air Force Junior ROTC program (or any other JROTC program) does not result in a college scholarship, it is a strong indicator of potential success with college level ROTC. Junior ROTC programs do not recruit for the Air Force or the other services; their mission is simply to "build better and more productive citizens." The program educates and trains high school cadets in citizenship, promotes community service, instills responsibility, character, and self-discipline, and provides instruction in air and space fundamentals. Presently, there are over 91,000 students enrolled in the Air Force Junior ROTC program. Students who participate in the JROTC programs do not incur any obligation to any of the Armed Services. The Junior ROTC program is open to all young people who are at least in the eighth grade, physically fit, and citizens of the United States.

AFROTC scholarship information

For more information about Air Force ROTC programs and scholarship applications, write to: Air Force ROTC, Recruiting Branch, 551 E. Maxwell Boulevard, Maxwell AFB, AL 36112-6106. See Appendix A for phone numbers and website address.

3

POSITION YOURSELF
FOR SUCCESS

You must effectively market yourself in order to win an ROTC scholarship. What may seem like a chaotic jumble of high school experiences can be reorganized to present an applicant who not only deserves an ROTC scholarship, but who would excel in the program. Applicants aren't awarded scholarships because they're team captains or have strong GPAs. They must arrange their experiences in a way that portrays them as deserving of a military scholarship.

Since the selection board's perception of you is the key factor in their decision, you must enhance that perception in order to maximize your chance of winning the scholarship. While completing the application, keep in mind the military perspective of the person reading it. The image you present as an applicant must appeal to this military perspective. Convey a sincere interest in the military and exhibit qualities that are important to them. Leadership, integrity, loyalty, and physical fitness are the most widely recognized qualities of military personnel. They take great pride in these qualities and, most importantly, they easily recognize and embrace people who share them. By demonstrating that you possess indications of these qualities, the selection board will consider you as an ideal candidate for the ROTC program.

Keep in mind that, comparatively, military personnel don't receive as much financial compensation for their work as many civilian workers do. Although living under such an unusually strict code of conduct and honor doesn't compensate for the lack of money, it does give them tremendous self-respect. They take great pride in their way of life. If you want to become a part of it, you must demonstrate this desire by not only emphasizing your appreciation of such qualities, but the fact that you recognize many of them within yourself.

Each year the number of ROTC scholarship applicants increases, while the availability of scholarships remains constant. As a result, the military services can afford to be selective in choosing their recipients. Today's applicant must have the qualities of tomorrow's military officer. Qualities such as leadership, discipline, and integrity comprise the foundation of a military officer. By recognizing and displaying these qualities, an applicant can present him or herself as the ideal choice. However, in order for an applicant to effectively display these qualities, he or she must exhibit them throughout the entire application process, from essay to interview.

Nobody knows your experiences and abilities better than you do. Take a close look at the experiences you've had over the last few years and ask yourself, "Where can I find examples of leadership, trust, and courage in my life?" You should incorporate the answer into your application. It will help make the decision to award you a scholarship as easy as possible for the selection board.

No guarantees

This book does not guaranty that you'll win a scholarship. If your grades and scores don't meet the minimum requirements as dictated by the various applications, this guide isn't going to help you—you won't even be considered for a scholarship. However, if you're among the thousands of applicants who meet the requirements, but don't stand out among your peers, then this guide may be your savior. By following some advice, you can learn how to market your personal qualities and recent accomplishments so that the selection board will appreciate and understand them.

Unpredictability

The ROTC selection process can be extremely unpredictable. While grades, SAT/ACT scores, and other quantitative factors contribute to the final decision, the selection board often acts arbitrarily. Sometimes an average applicant will win a scholarship over an above-average applicant. The cause for this decision may be a well-written essay or, perhaps, the eloquent words in a letter of recommendation. Whenever a decision process involves people, the chance for unpredictability exists. This unpredictability can work to your advantage if you're an average applicant. A strong essay may cause the selection board to distinguish you from countless other average applicants (the profiles of average and above-average applicants are presented in-depth in Chapter Four). Don't let average grades dissuade you from applying. You can enhance an average appearance by transforming it into something that will appeal to the selection board. Give the application process your best shot; you have nothing to lose and everything to gain.

Board members will review your essays, your recommendations, and your leadership experience. They will form opinions about your ability to succeed in the military environment based on only a few pieces of information. While you can't do much about your poor grades in chemistry during sophomore year, you can definitely influence the arbitrary side of the selection process and make up for any shortcomings. Crafting and focusing your application will create the influence you need to affect this arbitrary side.

Obviously, the board members don't know the real you. They only know who you are from what they read about you. As far as the board is concerned, how you appear in your application is who you really are. Translate your mundane responsibilities at work and school into terms your reader will relate to: leadership, trust, and loyalty. The possibilities are as endless as your experiences. You have complete control over the manner in which you present your experiences. Make sure that you maximize their potential.

So where do I go from here?

Start by giving this guide a thorough reading. The outlined strategy will give you the foundation you need to develop your own personal plan of attack. Get started on some of the administrative items, as it may take longer than you think to request applications, retake the SAT/ACT, pick who will write your letters of recommendation, and get in shape. Many applicants have difficulty writing the essay, but the examples and writing tips included in Chapter Ten should provide you with enough advice to remove most of the anxiety. As you're writing the essay, you'll also want to make sure that you're managing your recommendations effectively (this process is explained in-depth in Chapter Eleven). Once you've completed your applications and you've qualified for the scholarship, schedule interviews with the various service recruiters. The interview is your chance to show the selection board a face behind the name, a side of you that the application cannot. Once it's all finished, sit back and wait. The hard part is over.

Do your research

An important item to consider is your familiarity with the military. Obviously, having not been in the military, you're not expected to have a keen grasp of military life. However, firsthand research of the military will increase your appeal as an applicant.

Visit the real thing

Check out a military institution. Experience a firsthand look at military life and make mental notes about what appeals to you. Later, when you write your essay, include this information in order to prove that you are serious enough about winning a scholarship to drive a hundred miles to visit a military base. Showing that you have some military exposure can only help your chances. You will appear more serious about winning the scholarship than other candidates who never took the time to make such a visit. For example, one applicant was able to arrange spending a day on a local Air Force base with a friend of the family. He wrote about his experience and demonstrated an appreciation for military life. The following is an excerpt from his essay:

"...Through a friend of the family's I was able to arrange spending a day on an AFB in Virginia. I followed a Lieutenant Colonel around for the whole day, attending several squadron meetings and speaking with several officers who were once ROTC students themselves. That day made me truly realize how much I want to be a part of the U.S. military, but more importantly how much I want this ROTC scholarship." Steven R., Virginia.

By demonstrating that you have a particular interest in the military, you position yourself as the ideal ROTC applicant. If you visit a base and find that an aspect of military life impresses you, then write it down. Selection boards want applicants who understand the military lifestyle for which they are applying. Some advice: don't think that you have been exposed to aspects of the military through "Rambo" movies or M*A*S*H reruns. You want to appear as an applicant who sees beyond the fact that "military stuff is cool." It is cool, but find a specific facet of it that interests you and mention it. You're trying to win an expensive scholarship from the military. You should be specific in terms of your attraction to military life.

If you can, attend a local military air show or visit a nearby naval base. There are decommissioned naval ships on the east and west coasts that offer tours. If all else fails, call your local recruiter or ROTC unit and ask if you can spend a day in his office. He will be more than happy to oblige you and, in most cases, put you to work. These experiences will portray you as an exceptionally well-grounded applicant who understands the military. To convey your military exposure, the following comment would be appropriate in either the application essay or in the interview:

"I have experienced a small facet of the military through attending a military air show. The experience interested me a great deal in aviation and I would like the opportunity to pursue this career in the military."

Pay attention and learn

If you do visit a military base, pay close attention to the various jobs that you see during the day. There will be fighter pilots, infantry officers, computer programmers, engineers, meteorologists, air controllers, military police, surgeons, nurses, tank commanders, and airborne specialists. If you have a specific vocation that you want to pursue, try to get a good look at it. Pay attention to the details of the job and, as mentioned before, include that interest in your essay or interview. Board members like to see that you are already thinking about more than just winning the scholarship. They want to know what you're going to do with it.

4

WHO SHOULD APPLY FOR AN ROTC SCHOLARSHIP?

Okay, so you're eligible to apply for an ROTC scholarship. Should you apply? Are you the type of student that commonly applies? Eligibility requirements exist in order to ensure a certain caliber of applicants. Meeting the initial quality standard is a good sign and it should encourage you. However, most applicants have no problem meeting these requirements. Their only concern is how they compare to the other applicants. Essentially, they want to know if they have a chance to win this scholarship. They don't want to waste their time applying if there's a high probability of rejection. Recognize that if you are eligible to apply, your application is already competitive.

The average applicant for ROTC scholarships is between his or her junior and senior years in high school and has the following characteristics:

An average applicant:

- Has above a 3.0 GPA out of 4.0

- Has above an 1100 SAT and 24 ACT (composite)

- Is ranked in the upper half of graduating class

- Plays one sport, varsity or junior varsity

- Participates in one or two extracurricular activities

- Has been active in some community service

- Has served in leadership positions on or off school grounds

Average applicants don't have all of these characteristics, but usually a mix of them. Some applicants have a higher GPA and a lower SAT/ACT, or vice versa, but often the two balance out. Some applicants win scholarships with GPAs close to 3.0, but they usually have other qualities that outweigh the GPA.

Don't worry if you don't fit the mold of the average applicant. Chances are good that you have several accolades, and one of them will place you at the level of the other applicants. Participation in team sports is important and so are any leadership roles you had during your high school career—either in student government, sports, or other extracurricular activities. Whatever the activity, you must convey a level of accomplishment. Some students have little in-school activities due to participation in an out-of-school activity, such as martial arts. In this case, highlight the importance of this activity on a separate sheet of paper. Discuss how, through your dedication and discipline, you have gained more than what a school club could offer. You can then assert that these qualities will help you excel in their particular ROTC program.

What if your scores and level of activities are well above those of the average applicant? The statistics for the above-average candidate are as follows:

Above-average applicant:

- Has above a 3.5 GPA out of 4.0

- Has above a 1200 SAT and 29 ACT (composite)

- Ranks in the top twenty-five percent of graduating class

- Captain of a varsity team / JROTC billet holder

- Participates in two or more extracurricular activities

- Has been active in community service

- Has served in leadership positions on/off school grounds

- Has a high level of physical fitness

If you have the first two qualifications and one or more of the others, the selection board would consider you to be an above-average applicant. The GPA and SAT are key elements of the above-average applicant. If those numbers are high, and you can provide the selection board with evidence that you have displayed leadership ability, your chances for winning a scholarship are very good. However, these numbers alone will not guaranty you a scholarship.

Keep in mind that the selection board wants to see qualities that will enable you to lead members of today's Armed Forces. Applicants who have high test scores, but no leadership skills, are not what the board wants. The students with the highest scores are smart, but without sports or extracurricular activity, they often have poor leadership ability. The selection boards search for well-balanced applicants and they do not want bookworms. Because finding a well-balanced applicant can be difficult, ROTC selection boards will often choose an applicant with strong leadership potential over one with strictly academic promise. Their ultimate goal is to find an applicant with equal portions of both.

Remember that these selection boards have either (1) a full-length photograph of you, or (2) a required comment about your potential for physical fitness by your interviewer. If an applicant lists no athletic activities, the board will look at the photo or at the interviewer's comments and ask, "Why?" They will make their own conclusions, most of which are unfavorable (e.g., that you have no coordination or that others can't get along with you). While that may not be the case, if you have little or no athletic activities, you must address your athletic deficiency or the issue is left to the selection board to decide.

Since applicants are selected on the basis of so many different qualities, it's difficult to define the characteristics of a scholarship winner. However, the Army's statistics give a vague idea of recipient accolades.

Applicant profile of U.S. Army ROTC
scholarship winners for 1996-97

President of class..............................15%
Other class officers...........................55%
National Honor Society...................80%
Varsity Letter winners.....................87%
Varsity Team captains......................54%
Junior ROTC participants...............17%
Club presidents.................................29%
Statistics, U.S. Army

CAN THOSE NUMBERS BE RIGHT?

Don't let these statistics discourage you. Scholarship winners rarely have more than three of the above distinctions. In fact, some recipients can't claim any of them among their accomplishments. Although the Air Force, Navy, and Marine Corps don't publish statistics like these, it's safe to assume that the numbers are fairly similar. Generally speaking, the average GPA and SAT/ACT scores for all accepted applicants are roughly the same for every branch of the military. One reason for this similarity is that many of the applicants apply to more than one ROTC scholarship program.

As long as you display a balance between your physical and academic ability, your chances remain good. Applicants worry too much about matching up to statistics. Don't focus on what you are not—focus on what you are, and then market yourself like crazy.

THE TYPE OF APPLICANT THAT SELECTION BOARDS LOOK FOR

You've now seen profiles of the average and above-average applicants. Not surprisingly, applicant experiences don't widely differ. Most applicants are seventeen years of age, high school seniors, and they carry with them the token experiences of a four-year high school adventure. Rarely does the selection board see an application with experiences that they've never seen before. As a result, the presentation of your individual experience is what counts. The following is a list of important elements to any high school experience.

Balance

Generally, people with a well-balanced cadre of experiences can handle any obstacle placed before them. Hence, you should try to demonstrate a balance between your athletic and academic experiences. Because military success depends on ingenuity and creativity, the selection board actively looks for applicants that represent these qualities.

Discipline and dedication

Experiences that demonstrate your discipline and or dedication are key indicators that you can complete a four-year ROTC program. Look for activities that you have been doing for an extended period of time and stress your dedication to them. Also emphasize any level of achievement that your dedication has rendered. Remember that these are essential qualities for an officer.

Physical fitness

Since physical fitness is such an important part of ROTC programs, you should stress any and all athletic experiences. Athletics can range from individual exercise (e.g., jogging, biking, swimming, and skiing) to team sports. Athletics are a strong indicator of many important qualities. For example, sports participation denotes discipline, strength, coordination, determination, endurance, teamwork, and the ability to give and follow instructions. These are impressive qualities with which to be associated. Make sure that your activities indicate a high degree of fitness.

Desire

Understandably, the board looks for an applicant with a burning desire to become a part of an ROTC program. These are applicants who display a strong desire to not only join ROTC, but to become a part of the military as a whole. The board holds these applicants in high regard, and the reason is simple. Ask yourself, "If I were awarding scholarships, would I select someone with a high degree of excitement about my particular program, or someone with a lukewarm attitude?"

One applicant, who had wanted a Navy/USMC ROTC Option scholarship, was rejected his first time around. The young man decided to wait and reapply the next year. In the meantime, he enlisted in the USMC Reserves, went to Boot Camp, and, during the interim, took a few community college courses. This young man barely met the minimum GPA/SAT requirements, but his desire to win an ROTC scholarship was unmatched and it paid off for him.

S-p-e-l-l i-t o-u-t

The selection board doesn't want to read between the lines of your essay and contemplate your ROTC success potential. They have thousands of applications to read and don't have the energy to strain ambiguous information. Give them what they're looking for right up front. Ask yourself, "What does the board want to see in my experience?" Then, ensure that each facet of your application, from essay to interview, fills that need. For example, don't be shy with your interviewer; tell him or her exactly what you want the selection board to know about you. Write it down on a note card if necessary, and bring it to the interview. Tell the interviewer to excuse your note card, but that you are a bit nervous and you want to make sure that you don't forget to tell him or her something important.

So what does the board want to see? Consider the following applicant stories.

A LOOK AT TWO APPLICANTS

It may be helpful for you to consider the situations of other applicants in comparison to yourself. This comparison may help you understand whom, besides yourself, applies for these scholarships. While everyone has a unique story to tell, the following two applicant sketches are based on elements from various applicants:

Applicant One

Laura's application differed slightly from others before the board. She had worked most of her adolescent life at an after school job to help with the family's bills. Although she had athletic potential, her high school was small and without many women's sports teams. As a result, Laura was the only girl to play soccer on the men's team. Her entire application indicated that she was a tough and determined girl. From her personal statement, it became obvious that she really wanted an ROTC scholarship. She didn't have a 4.0 GPA. At a 3.1, she was barely above the minimum requirements. At 1120, her SATs were also fairly average. However, she did have a strong sense of maturity and drive—qualities that, in the right context, can outweigh an SAT score. She had none of the accolades common to above-average applicants, and few in-school leadership positions to mention. But because of the way she presented her achievements and goals, Laura was awarded a scholarship. She beat out plenty of her peers who had much higher numbers and more honors. How did she do it?

Her essay showed a clear understanding of her position as an average applicant and focused on why her scores were *not* reflective of her ability to excel in ROTC. She showed a sincere enthusiasm for the scholarship program that wasn't seen among the other applicants. She explained how her decision to help support her family often came before her schoolwork. Although she was distressed about the average appearance of her application, she was not ashamed of her family commitment. This commitment had not given her academic distinctions, but it had instilled in her the qualities necessary for ROTC success. She incorporated her strong desire to be in the military and how important it was for her to reach her goal of winning a scholarship. Her candid approach profoundly impressed the selection board, resulting in a scholarship offer.

Applicant Two

Steve, on the other hand, was an applicant who seemed to have it all: 1400 SAT, 3.8 GPA, captain of the football team, and student government leader. He ranked in the upper levels of applicants and appeared to have few obstacles in his path to a scholarship. However, his personal statement contained a nonchalance that changed that view. Shockingly, in his own words, he stated that he "wasn't really sure if [he] wanted to be in the military." If you're trying to win an enormous scholarship from the military, why would you express your reservations about serving in it? The military strictly avoids potential program dropouts. Even if you are in the upper echelon of applicants, if you express the slightest inclination of uncertainty, it will ruin your scholarship chances. The scholarship was offered to someone else who expressed a clear desire for it. Ask yourself, "If I were a board member and only had a handful of scholarships to grant, to which type of applicant would I award it? You would give it to a student who knows what he or she wants and won't waste taxpayers' money by dropping out of the scholarship program.

So, who should apply for these scholarships? As long as students meet the necessary requirements and understand their obligations, they should apply. The elements of the average and above-average applicants were listed not to dissuade you from applying, but to let you know where you stand when it comes time to put together the application. If you recognize that you are an average applicant, then you know that you have to write a really strong essay and impress the interviewer (not that you shouldn't do this anyway). You need to know when to put in the extra effort in order to make an average application stand out.

If you find commonalities between yourself and the above-average applicants, you should still work hard on your essay and interview. Generally, all applicants are smart, athletic and want to be in the military. As the two applicant sketches indicate, the factor that separates you from others rests in the way you present yourself. Again, the application process is not cut and dry. If you meet the requirements, then apply! You can always craft your experiences to demonstrate your strong fit with ROTC.

5

DIVERSITY IN ROTC

If you are a minority, the ROTC selection board will pay special attention to your application. As a minority, you belong to a group that is underrepresented in the U.S. military. As the proportion of ethnicity in our country changes, the military must follow suit. Unfortunately, this proportional adjustment doesn't happen automatically. It takes careful consideration and planning to increase the number of women and minorities in the military, and even more consideration to retain them. In terms of the ROTC program, the military realizes that it must train a more diverse group of officers who will be comfortable leading a military with the ethnic composition of our country.

How does a minority status affect my application?

A minority status will affect your application, but the degree to which it does is up to you. By indicating that you're a minority, your application will receive extra consideration. However, if you discuss the effect your ethnicity or gender has had on your development as a student leader, then your minority status could affect your application to a much greater degree. The personal statement and interview provide opportunities for you to discuss this effect.

As a minority, your upbringing and development have most likely been affected in some way and you should comment on it. For example, if you're a female and you feel that you have been denied the opportunity for leadership, then you could emphasize your untapped potential. Elaborating on your experiences as a minority or a female (and how those experiences will help your transformation into an officer) will differentiate you from other applicants.

However, if you're a minority and feel that this status hasn't affected you in any noticeable way, then avoid the minority issue. If it's something that you do not feel strongly about, then do not force the issue or exaggerate an incident of ethnic inequality. Be honest in your interview and essay because the selection board can see straight through empty words.

Remember that, by its nature, the military is very conservative. With that said, the ROTC application is not the place to voice your discontent with the racial inequalities of America. Yes, racial inequalities do exist, but the ROTC application is not the best place to address them. The scholarship selection boards are actively looking to increase the number of women and minorities in their services, but they are not looking for radical students. Although you should underscore your unique ethnicity, you should also highlight your ability to fit in with other ethnic groups. Regardless of ethnicity or gender, military officers must be able to work together. Expressing this capability is an important facet of a minority application.

No GUARANTEES

A final word about applying for ROTC scholarships with a minority status: this status alone will not guaranty you a scholarship. Every other element of your application must be just as competitive as the rest of the applicant pool. There must be indications of athletic ability, student leadership, discipline, and ambition. Your status as part of a minority group is important to the military, but it is not the only factor. As long as you know who you are and what you would like to become, the military will be very interested in you. After all, diversity represents reality.

6

THE IMPORTANCE
OF THE SAT/ACT

As if you haven't heard how standardized tests can influence your life, this chapter will explain their influence in yet another area. Taking the SAT or ACT is a necessary evil, as almost all colleges require these scores as part of the application process. While this guide isn't going to give you test-taking strategies, it can offer you some tips and suggestions. There are several major organizations that give you the inside track on the SAT and ACT through books and courses. Their contact information will appear later in this chapter. However, in terms of the SAT and ACT in relation to the ROTC scholarship process, here are some suggestions.

TAKE THE TEST EARLY

Often students try to do everything at once: apply to colleges, apply for ROTC scholarships, and study for the SAT or ACT. Even if you were a genius, you might still neglect one of the three for the sake of the other two. Something will undoubtedly get the short end of your attention and, more often than not, it's the SAT or ACT. As painful as these tests are, preparing for them can raise your scores dramatically. Higher test scores will not only increase your chances of winning a scholarship, but also your chances of being admitted to a good college. Consequently, you should avoid shortchanging yourself on preparation time by taking the test before the application process begins.

The selection board has no preference over which of the two tests you take, provided that you do well on whichever one you choose. The Electronic Testing Service (ETS) offers the SAT four times a year in major cities throughout the United States. There are plans to move the SAT to a computer-based, adaptive test, which may influence your decision. You can find brochures about the SAT and ACT in your high school's career center or guidance counselor's office. You can also request them directly from ETS. The score you receive on standardized tests is valid for five years. If you get to college and want to transfer, or reapply to another ROTC program, you do not have to retake the exam.

AN SAT/ACT SCORE IS ONLY
PART OF THE WHOLE PICTURE

These standardized tests do not reflect your ability to become a good military officer. They are exercises that contain analogies, vocabulary, reading comprehension, algebra, and geometry. You've probably covered most of the material in your high school classes. It's important to recognize that your SAT/ACT scores are only one of the several elements that the ROTC selection board will consider when reviewing your application. The ROTC scholarship process is very similar to the college admissions process that considers the GPA and SAT in addition to other aspects of your application. In fact, in its ROTC scholarship information handouts, the Air Force discusses its "whole-person" approach to selecting applicants. To further support this assertion, take a look at the various required recommendations. All the different elements that constitute your application paint a picture of you that a standardized test can hardly match. Selection board members are interested in grades and scores, but only in order to qualify you as an acceptable applicant. Once you pass this initial hurdle, your other accomplishments must prove your worth.

PRACTICE PAYS OFF

Practicing for the standardized tests is one of the most time consuming things you will do in the college application process. However, you will be rewarded from the practice. It's commonplace for students who take a preparation course, or buy one of the home preparation books, to increase their scores by at least one hundred points. Test preparation companies make guarantees to their students of sizable improvements, and commit full use of their facilities until the student raises his or her score. Kaplan is a test preparation company that makes this guarantee. For example, their guaranteed margin of improvement is eighty points for the SAT. If your scores don't increase by at least that much, you can continue to use their testing center until they do.

The material covered in the SAT is not that difficult. Students tend to think that the math section borders on astrophysics, but that's simply not true. You were probably exposed to most of the material by the time you were sixteen. It's the way that the test presents the questions that makes them so formidable. By practicing for the test and reviewing appropriate material, you'll become intimately familiar with the format of the exam. This familiarity is critical to performing well on the exam. After taking five to ten practice exams, you will start to notice obvious patterns in the questions.

To perform well on these tests, you need to have a basic understanding of their content, you need to hone the thinking and testing skills that underlie the SAT and ACT, and you need to know their nature. Content and skills are obviously important, but understanding the nature of these tests (i.e., their set-up, structure, and tricks) will allow you to gain points that you might not otherwise have earned.

Understand that the SAT and ACT don't measure intelligence (nor do they even accurately predict college performance), but they do measure test-taking skills (with some verbal and mathematical prerequisite knowledge, to be sure). The more preparation and study you pursue, the more these skills improve, while pre-test panic and anxiety decline. Test-taking is a skill that will develop your mental endurance and thought process. Where before you would come to a certain type of geometry question and stare blankly at the page, after seeing this type of question a few times, it will not be a big deal. Also, this familiarity will save time when it comes to actually taking the exam. You will not waste time reading the directions for each section, because you will already know what is required of you. You will be able to begin immediately. Any time you save in not reading the directions can be spent answering more questions and reviewing your work.

TAKE AN SAT REVIEW COURSE

There is no getting around it. If you want to increase your score on the SAT, you're going to have to spend some money on a review course. Test preparation courses can cost anywhere from three hundred to eight hundred dollars. If a student who took a five hundred-dollar course improves his or her score by one hundred points, quick math will tell you that the improvement came at a cost of five dollars per point. That is a small price to pay considering that it may be the difference in qualifying you for an enormous scholarship.

On the other hand, books by Kaplan, Princeton Review, and ARCO are less expensive than a class (twenty to forty dollars), but their effect on your scores depends entirely on the effort you put into them. Conceivably, you can get the same strategies from one of these books as you can from a more expensive course, but people who take courses usually have an easier time staying on track with the lessons. On your own with a book, you may become distracted and lose focus. Your level of preparation should reflect the importance that the ROTC scholarship represents to you. If you consider the test preparation costs in relation to the benefits of a huge scholarship and college admission, they are fairly reasonable.

GO TO THE PROFESSIONALS

Can you teach yourself the test-taking strategies of the SAT or ACT? If you're a gifted test-taker and the testing concepts come easily to you, then you might not need a preparation course. However, most students prefer to have these strategies presented in a classroom setting. The test preparation companies earn their living providing you with the information needed to achieve a better score on the SAT/ACT. They will tutor you until you improve your score. After all, it is what you're paying them for. If you don't perform well, then it reflects poorly on them. Some good sources to call for SAT preparation assistance:

CLASSES

Stanley Kaplan, 1-800-KAP TEST or 527-8378

Classes are good and all the instructors must score above the ninetieth percentile on the exam in order to teach the course. Kaplan has one of the most extensive libraries of practice tests and instructional tapes. Fees include all take-home study materials.

Princeton Review, 1-800-995-5585

This course usually costs less than Kaplan's course, and often makes the classes and the material fun to learn. They have a practical attitude towards taking the exam, and often toss in some occasional humor. Fees include all take-home study materials.

Books

Kaplan ACT, 1999 ed. Simon & Schuster
Cost < $20.00

Kaplan recognizes that stress reduction is just as important as knowledge and problem-solving when taking standardized tests. This guidebook is an impressive mix of clear, demystifying information about the test and relaxation tips that would also be valuable for politicians, business executives, or anyone who's ever had a bad day.

Notable features include a set of instructions and time lines for using the book (including the "Classic" two-month plan and the "Panic" two-week plan), a complete timed test, and the "Kaplan Advantage Stress Management System." The individual "Skill-Building Workout" sections for English, math, reading, and science reasoning are all easily digestible and contain many practical tips for improving scores. The strategic summaries at the end of each section are particularly helpful in reiterating what you should focus on. They also include some very solid practice tests with thorough explanations. Kaplan guides have writing that is snappy and fun, making this test preparation an enjoyable read.

Arco ACT SuperCourse, 1998 ed. MacMillian
Cost < $20.00

Arco puts together strong test preparation materials, which goes for their SAT preparation book as well. They break down the anatomy of the test and present understandable strategies with helpful hints. They offer three full-length practice tests and boast more practice questions than any other guide.

Kaplan SAT & PSAT, 1999 ed. Simon & Schuster
Cost < $20.00

Kaplan SAT & PSAT 1999 is a good standardized test guide for a number of reasons. For one, Kaplan has been in the business of helping students prepare for standardized tests since the 1930s, so they know what you need to learn and how to best impart that information. Also, they understand high school students, so the text is written with students' study habits, preferences, and concerns in mind. For each test section, there are plenty of practice questions, followed by a discussion of why one answer is correct, why the other answers are wrong, and how best to arrive at the correct answer. They teach paraphrasing skills, skimming, and quantitative comparisons. They instruct how to prepare if you've started months in advance, and what you can learn if you've waited until the last minute. With additional chapters on stress management systems, study aids, and college-admission essays, Kaplan

provides a great service to the college-bound student.
Arco SAT SuperCourse, 3rd ed. MacMillian
Cost < $20.00

Arco's popular SuperCourse for the SAT is now completely updated for the new test format in effect as of March 1994. Special features include unique "walk-through" test-taking drills, eye-catching graphics, hundreds of "inside" strategies, full-length practice tests, and more. Their book contains two, full-length SATs along with detailed explanations. They focus heavily on mastering the fundamentals of the test and do a good job of highlighting the skills necessary to succeed in each section.

The Princeton Review, Cracking the SAT/PSAT, 1999 ed. Random House, Cost < $30.00

This book comes complete with a CD-ROM that contains four sample tests and detailed explanations. The inclusive CD-ROM is a great feature, and enough to warrant buying this book (as if its presence on the New York Times Bestseller list isn't good enough). The book has chapters on how to beat the test's individual sections as well as a strong focus on vocabulary.

Any questions about the exam?

The test preparation company you are using can usually answer any questions you have about the exam. However, if you have some administrative questions about the SAT or ACT, feel free to give ETS a call. They are in New Jersey at 1 (609) 771-7330.

These suggestions about the standardized tests are offered to facilitate the process for you. While it takes tremendous effort, preparing for the SAT and ACT can improve your score by hundreds of points. This improvement not only affects your college admission process, but can also make you more appealing in the eyes of the selection board.

A final few words: don't be frightened by the test. The selection boards place a great deal of importance on the other elements of your application: essays, recommendations, extracurricular activities, community involvement, leadership ability, and character. All of these factors contribute to their final decision. Your standardized test score adds to the final, complete picture of you, but it's only one element in the many that will define you. Study like crazy, do your best, and move on.

7

ROTC UNIT AND COLLEGE VISITS

If you want to maximize your chances of winning a scholarship, then it's a great idea to visit the ROTC unit of your school of choice. When you decide which school you want to attend, give the unit commander a phone call. Let him know that you are applying for the ROTC scholarship and that you would like to meet him and ask him some questions. There are several reasons why this visit can be worth your effort.

The U.S. Military knows that it needs a certain amount of new ROTC officers matriculating through their system each year in order to supply new lieutenants to each branch of service. These needs are translated into quotas. Each branch of service counts on these quotas in order to estimate the number of personnel they will have in the coming year. It is vital that these quotas are met. Any inability to meet these quotas can negatively impact the careers of the unit commanders in charge of those quotas.

These quotas are handed down to ROTC units in the form of numbers. They are guidelines for the ROTC unit commanders to let them know if they are meeting the over-all goals of the military. For example, a quota might be given to the unit commander of a medium-sized university, dictating that each year that particular school must have twenty-five commission-seeking officer candidates graduate per year, or a total of one hundred active students at any given time. If, for some reason, this unit commander's numbers are below his required quota, he will do everything in his power to correct them.

Imagine how difficult it is for the commander of an ROTC unit to recruit new members during the school year. Students are busy with schoolwork, they're busy with their social lives, and they're not too interested in the physical demands placed on cadets. Now, imagine what a relief it is for this unit commander to receive a phone call from someone like yourself, who shows a genuine interest in his program. This commander will go out of his way to get you to join his unit because it's in his best interest. If you need any assistance in completing your application, or are looking for material to write in your essay, give an ROTC unit a call. It can only help you.

Let's say that you are an average applicant whose application really needs a boost to make you distinct from the countless other average applicants. A visit to an ROTC unit can portray you as an unique applicant. Just as visiting a local military base demonstrates your high degree of interest to the board, a visit to an ROTC unit is one step further than that. This visit would present you as a serious applicant. If it is difficult for you to visit an ROTC unit, then you can communicate with them in other ways. The point is that you want to show the ROTC selection board that you have taken the time to visit an ROTC unit and that you understand what it's all about. This task is not difficult, and yet only a handful of applicants will display this effort in a given year.

What if you don't get a scholarship this time around? Don't worry, it's not the end of the world. If you apply the next year, you will be considered in an entirely different category. If you don't win the scholarship and choose to attend a college with an ROTC unit, you can apply midway through your freshman year for a scholarship that will cover the next two or three years. Your chances are much better in these selection committees because there are fewer applicants. Never lose sight of your goal, because there's always a way.

Keeping in contact with the ROTC unit commander at your school will maximize your chances when you reapply. In fact, this unit commander will most likely be the official interviewer for your application. If you have a good working relationship with the officer in charge of the ROTC unit, he will do everything in his power to grant you one of the unit's slots as they become available. Students do drop out of ROTC. Poor grades, drugs, and lack of determination weed out the weak ones, leaving many open slots as the year progresses. The unit Officer in Charge (OIC) must fill these slots, and if the OIC knows of your interest, you will become a prime candidate for a slot.

Often times, these OICs will put together your package during your freshman year. Because of the close relationship between you and the unit commander, the OIC will most likely facilitate your application at every step of the selection process. You should never give up hope of winning one of these scholarships. Let your intentions be known, show your sincerity, and people will take care of you.

8

PHYSICAL READINESS

O kay, so you're applying for an ROTC scholarship. Has it occurred to you that some services require a basic physical fitness exam? This test may be comprised of physical exercises or may simply compare your height and weight against those of the national average. If you fall within an acceptable range, you are considered fit. If you do not meet the weight standards assigned to your height, it may prevent you from winning a scholarship. The notion of passing a physical fitness exam may sound obvious to you, but many applicants pass this test with marginal performance. Marginal is not average in the military—it is below average. You must show the selection board that you respect them, their service, and the ROTC program enough to sufficiently pass this test.

OVER-TRAIN

Don't just train for these tests—over-train. If you have to do a one and a half-mile run, then practice running two miles. Always train with a harder amount than the test requires. This over-training applies to everything: push-ups, pull-ups, sit-ups, and shuttle runs. When the day of fitness exam arrives, it will ease your mind to know that you can do more than they want. It also looks good on your application to see that you are in top physical condition.

How do I know which physical tests to practice?

The average test consists of basic physical fitness requirements that are intended to highlight people who are physically unable to perform under military standards.

THE TESTS

Air Force:

Although in the past the Air Force has not required a physical fitness test for its ROTC scholarship applicants, there is some talk that this may change in the near future. The best way to meet this potential challenge is to be prepared to take the standard Air Force physical fitness test. This test has the following requirements:

	Sit-ups	Push-ups	2 mile run
Males:	44	30	18 minutes
Females:	41	9	21 minutes

Army:

The Army Physical Fitness Test is given to all scholarship winners when they enroll in college in the fall. Scholarship benefits will not begin until you have successfully passed the Army PFT. This fitness test consists of repetitive push-ups and sit-ups and a two mile run. Good physical conditioning is critical to performing well on this test. Generally:

- A male between 17 and 21 years of age should arrive at college able to do 42 push-ups, a female 18 push-ups.

- A male needs to be able to do 52 sit-ups and a female 50 sit-ups.

- A good time for the two mile run for a male would be 16 minutes and for a female 19 minutes.

NAVY:

Currently, the U.S. Navy has no physical fitness requirement for ROTC scholarships. The physical fitness of each applicant is judged by their appearance as well as their level of sports-related activity.

MARINES:

Marine Option applicants are required to take a standard Marine Corps physical fitness test. This test consists of pull-ups (maximum of twenty), sit-ups (maximum of one hundred), and a three-mile run. Applicants are not expected to ace the test. It serves as a measuring tool for an applicant's general physical condition.

Generally, the physical fitness tests are required after you have been awarded a scholarship. For more details, contact your local recruiter and tell him or her that you are applying for the ROTC scholarship. Ask what types of physical tests you will be required to pass in order to apply, and he or she will explain them to you. Make sure you understand how you are to perform the tests. If there is anything that you don't understand, ask for clarification. You will most likely have to set up an appointment with the recruiter to take this fitness test. Prepare for this test well ahead of time, as it will drastically improve your performance.

9

HOW TO FILL OUT
AN APPLICATION

Each military service has an ROTC application that meets Department of Defense (DOD) guidelines. Standard questions can range from ethnicity to past drug use. The answers to these questions paint an essential picture of the applicant for the selection board. While most questions on the application are routine, and therefore require little comment, there are a few questions that require more attention. The manner in which you approach these questions could make or break your application. Some of these questions are designed to raise red flags of warning when checked "yes" by an applicant.

Ever been arrested?

Invariably, every ROTC application will contain a question asking if you have ever been in trouble with the law. Its order of appearance indicates its importance in the selection process. Usually, it's one of the first questions on the application. By addressing this issue right away, the selection board can deal with a situation that might disqualify an applicant from the selection process.

If a traffic violation was your only brush with the law, then this information will not affect you. However, if you've had other troubles with the law, your response to this question should be carefully written. Your description of the incident is the only chance you'll have to explain yourself. Put some time and consideration into your remarks.

If you were charged with a misdemeanor, like vandalism, give a complete description of the incident, the nature of the offense, and a brief comment about what you learned from the incident. Normally, a single misdemeanor on your record will not ruin your chances for a scholarship. However, any criminal incident, whether its minor or not, does prompt deliberation by the selection board. Your explanation must remove any concern that the description of the incident may generate.

If your brush with the law was a felony offense, such as drug possession with the intent to sell, the situation becomes much more serious. Felony incidents include serious crimes that usually indicate a troubled individual. Unless a credible explanation exists for the incident, a past felony makes it difficult for the military to accept you. However, do not let a felony offense discourage you. If the selection board sees evidence that you have cleaned up your act since then, they may give you a chance. Remember, when it's justified, the selection board can make uncommon decisions.

The application asks that you address any incident in the remarks section provided. Do not feel confined to this small space. They expect an explanation, but they don't want to read your microscopic handwriting crammed into the small remarks section. Always prepare a typed page for your remarks and clip it to the application when it's submitted. If you present the incident as a learning experience, or possibly an accident, the selection board may ignore it and give you the benefit of the doubt. Don't be afraid of your past. Take responsibility for your mistakes and explain your actions; it may serve as an opportunity for you to demonstrate your integrity.

DON'T LIKE GUNS?

Every application will have a question that can be described as "moral conflict." In other words, "Do you have any moral obligation [like religion or personal belief] that will prevent you from conscientiously bearing arms and supporting or defending the Constitution of the United States from all enemies, foreign and domestic?" Or this can be translated as: "Do you foresee a problem with picking up a weapon [which you may have to fire at another person] in order to defend your country?" If you do have a moral problem with bearing arms, it will probably interfere with the success of your application. Many people cannot bring themselves to raise a weapon against another human being, no matter what the circumstances. This refusal to bear arms is obviously a problem when applying for a position in the military and needs to be dealt with immediately in order to remove all doubt. A check in the "yes" box requires considerable supplemental explanation, while a check in the "no" box is simply routine.

MILITARY STATUS OF PARENTS

Were either of your parents ever in the U.S. Military? If they were, it might help your scholarship chances. ROTC applications usually have a section that asks about the military status of your parents. A parent with military experience signals to the selection board that you should understand certain aspects of military duty. To the selection board, you are a good bet for not dropping out of an ROTC program. Thousands of dollars in scholarship money are wasted every year on

ROTC cadets who drop out of the program. The military reacts poorly to dropouts and tries to identify and avoid them early on.

This section will also ask if you have any relatives (e.g., brothers, sisters, or cousins) in ROTC programs. Again, an affirmative answer to this question indicates the likelihood of your success to the selection board. If your relatives have successfully completed ROTC training, then the selection board feels that, if given the chance, you will likely succeed in an ROTC program.

YOUR PRIOR MILITARY SERVICE

Did you enlist in the military and then decide that you wanted to go back to school? ROTC scholarships are frequently awarded to prior service members who meet various guidelines. Each ROTC application inquires about prior military service. They enjoy awarding scholarships to these applicants and for good reason. It's highly probable that prior service members will honor the scholarship contract. They will most likely finish four years of a college ROTC program and serve the required number of years as an active duty officer. Because of the ultra-high success rate of prior service members, these applicants are highly regarded and often receive first consideration when the voting process begins. In the eyes of the board, these applicants served their country honorably and deserve the chance to attend college. These applicants are also considered special because of their scarcity, often representing less than two-percent of the applicant pool.

Do you have a minority background?

Are you a minority? The military sets aside a certain number of scholarships every year for minority applicants. Although indicating your ethnic background is optional on most applications, do not be afraid to indicate that you are considered a minority. It may increase your chances of winning a scholarship. (Refer back to Chapter Five, "Diversity in ROTC").

Is this your second time applying?

Did you apply last year and get rejected? Are you now a freshman or sophomore in college applying for a second time? ROTC applications usually include a short question that covers past application attempts. The selection board wants to know your application history for two good reasons:

1. They will look at the application that you previously submitted and try to deduce why you weren't accepted.

2. It tells them that you are an applicant who seriously wants a scholarship. Your effort to reapply emphasizes your dedication.

If this section applies to you, don't hide past application attempts. The fact that you are reapplying will most likely place you in a position to be admitted over a more qualified, first-time applicant. Explain your situation as required by the application, with your remarks on a separate, typed piece of paper. Use the opportunity to mention the reason for which you are reapplying (i.e., how much you want to be a part of ROTC).

Shotgun approach

Are you applying to multiple ROTC scholarship programs? Applications usually ask to which other ROTC programs you are applying. Some words of advice: select their particular program and leave the remainder of the fill-in circles empty. As a result of what is known as "inter-service rivalry," some service members feel threatened by other services. If you admit that you are applying for more than one program, it may indicate that you either don't have a clear idea of what you want to do in the military or that you have no loyalty to their service. Remember that they appreciate and understand loyalty.

Board members may view your shotgun approach as an indicator that you may defer their offer of a scholarship should you receive one. They would rather give it to someone who truly wants it, rather than someone who will try their program for a year and then transfer into another program. Although this notion of inter-service jealousy sounds ridiculous, it happens, and it may affect your application. Again, if you are applying to more than one ROTC program, you are better off leaving the remainder of the fill-in circles empty. With this approach, you avoid dishonesty as well as any possibility of inter-service issues.

Drug statement

In every case, ROTC applications will ask you to make an official statement about your relationship with illicit drugs. If you have never used drugs before, simply answer the questions. If, on the other hand, you have experimented with drugs and have officially admitted to doing so in front of a military official, your chances of earning an ROTC scholarship are slim. At the beginning of any discussion about an applicant, the fact that he or she has used drugs will surface immediately. Aside from criminal charges, the issue is considered with more importance than any other aspect of the individual application. With most selection boards, if an applicant admits to past drug use, the results are not favorable. You can have the highest honors and the most attractive application, but if you admit to the board that you have been caught using drugs, they will most likely vote against you. Past drug use indicates the possibility of future use. It doesn't matter if you insist that you only tried drugs once and that you'll never do it again; the fact that you've used them sends a warning to the board. The board is entrusted to make sure that these scholarships are awarded to students who won't waste the government's time and the taxpayers' money. College offers plenty of temptations for young adults, and the board wants an applicant who shows resistance to temptation. Selection board members take their responsibility of finding trustworthy young adults very seriously.

Once you're in the military, either as a member of an ROTC unit or active duty, you will be governed by a "zero tolerance" policy for illegal drug use. Anyone caught using drugs faces an Other Than Honorable (OTH) service discharge. When an applicant for a sizable scholarship shows even the slightest drug history, the military becomes extremely cautious and closely examines that applicant. It's not unheard of for an applicant that only "experimented" with drugs to be awarded a scholarship, but the rest of the application is heavily scrutinized.

Activity matrix

This section of the application demonstrates your history of involvement in activities throughout high school. By merely scanning the items you fill in, the selection board can grasp your level of involvement and any leadership positions you've held. The design of the matrix encourages the applicant to record as many activities as he or she can remember.

Mark every activity that you were involved in during high school. Some applicants mistakenly think to themselves, "I only attended half of that activity's meetings. I don't want to appear as a person who spreads himself/herself too thin. I'll just put down the activities that I devoted serious time to and omit the others." This line of thought is incorrect. Without a doubt, you should include all your activities. The Air Force, Navy, and Marine Corps use the level of your extracurricular involvement to rank you against other applicants. The more activities you have on the matrix, the higher your ranking will be. The selection board uses a point system wherein each activity contributes points towards your ranking (discussed in-depth later). The bottom line is that by indicating all your high school activities, you are positioning yourself for a scholarship.

Intended college major

Are you ready for a good hint? Some services, such as the Air Force, require you to declare your intended major. This piece of information is critical to your application's success for one reason: the Air Force conducts its selection boards based on majors. For example, all Electrical Engineering majors are put into a group and evaluated together (let's say there are five hundred of them). Now, the Air Force may only have fifty

ROTC scholarships for Electrical Engineers in that given year. Therefore, only fifty out of those five hundred applicants could be offered scholarships. Thus, your success depends upon your declared major.

Are you ready for an even better hint? Logically, many Air Force applicants want to be pilots and, understandably, most of them believe that the only way to become a pilot is to declare a major in Aeronautical or Aerospace Engineering. Although this belief makes perfect sense, it's a big mistake. Let's say that in a given year, there are 5,000 applicants for AFROTC scholarships. Of those, 5,000 applicants, 2,000, or forty-percent of them, indicate that their intended major is Aeronautical or Aerospace Engineering. So, there are 2,000 applicants in the Aeronautical or Aerospace Engineering group, while the remaining 3,000 are evenly divided among the thirteen other recognized majors (including all the Non-Technical majors grouped as one major). Well, the Air Force may only have a quota for one hundred aeronautical engineers and one hundred aerospace engineers. Therefore, the total number of aerospace engineers is only two hundred. Those two hundred are selected from the 2,000 total aerospace applicants, which translates to a measly ten-percent acceptance rate. In contrast, the other non-aerospace majors might have selection rates of twenty to thirty percent. The idea is to choose a major that will not be as saturated as Aerospace Engineering. However, determining which majors the Air Force will need is the hard part. Some majors, like Mechanical and Electrical Engineering are always good bets, while others, like Chemical Engineering, might not receive any scholarships for allocation in a given year.

The important thing to realize is that several majors, such as Computer Science or Mechanical Engineering, have just as good of a chance of becoming pilots out of college as

Aeronautical or Aerospace Engineering majors. If your application is in one of the non-aerospace piles, you will have a higher probability of being selected than you would in Aeronautical or Aerospace Engineering. So how do you determine which major to select? Talk with your ROTC recruiter and ask him: "Which majors are needed this year?" "Which majors were needed last year?" "Do they expect the trend to continue this year?" Although the recruiters are not supposed to reveal this type of information, they may help you if they like you.

FORMAT FOR RECOMMENDATIONS AND COMMENTS

Although this book dedicates an entire chapter to the issue of recommendations, a brief overview is appropriate. Recommendations provide critical support for the positioning and focus of your application. If your essay asserts that you have strong leadership skills and a keen interest in aviation, then it's crucial that your recommendations support these assertions. The selection board takes these letters very seriously, so careful thought should go into who writes them and what they contain. It's important to select people who know you well enough to make a strong testament to your abilities and potential as a U.S. Military officer (discussed in depth later). While a recommendation from a prominent town figure may seem impressive to you, if this person barely knows you and discusses your qualities in non-specific terms, it will not impress the board. Board members look for thoughtful, well-written recommendations from people who can vouch for your leadership, management, and academic abilities.

MATH AND ENGLISH TEACHER EVALUATIONS

After four years of high school, there must be at least one English and one math teacher who like you. However, if you don't get along with them or if they don't know your name, you should probably begin improving their perception of you. It's important for the board to get an idea of your writing and analytical skills because these skills are vital to success in the military. Reviewing your teachers' comments is a sure way for the board to becomes familiar with your ability. While these recommendations are not as weighty as your GPA and SAT/ACT scores, one poor comment can raise warning signs for a selection board.

Board members want to obtain many different perspectives on your abilities and personality. Request recommendations from people who know you in different ways. For example, you might reserve one recommendation for your manager at work. If that isn't possible, try to find a family friend who has prior military service and can make a comment similar to the following: "As a veteran myself, I know firsthand that Jim would make a fine officer because ...etc." These perspectives help the selection board to better understand you. Your essays, interviews, and recommendations offer a telling self-portrait. This portrait appears more complete if those writing your recommendations can describe different aspects of your character.

Some recommendations have the best intent, but they are poorly written and reflect unfavorably on the applicant. Make sure you select a person who can write well. The style and content of these letters reflects upon you and on the quality of your application. There are ways to ensure the quality of your recommendations. When you give them the recommendation form, tell these people exactly what you require of them. They will want to help you, but may not understand what the military looks for in an applicant. Therefore, make sure that you:

- Fill out all the sections that are not required of the person writing the letter of recommendation.

- Take some time and discuss how important this opportunity will be for you. Tell them what you want to do in the military and why.

- Be straightforward and tell them that in order to win this scholarship, your qualities of leadership, integrity, and maturity must be addressed. Ask them to mention these qualities in their comments. If you have to, write these qualities on a piece of paper and attach it to the recommendation.

- Military personnel are conditioned to ranking each other in a numerical manner. The selection board will understand an applicant's potential better if they can see him or her ranked against his or her peers. Ask your teachers to rank your ability to succeed in the military out of all the students he or she has encountered. For example, "In my math class of twenty-five students, I would rank John's ability in the top three."

- Include a pre-addressed, pre-stamped envelope with the recommendation form.

- Tell them the date when they must submit the recommendation.

THE MOST COMMON PEOPLE SELECTED
TO WRITE LETTERS OF RECOMMENDATION

- The applicant's employer who can comment on any managerial promise that the applicant has displayed. For example, "Johnny is the head stock boy of the grocery store and supervises three co-workers."

- The coach of the applicant's athletic team who can comment on the leadership skills that the applicant displays on the field and the respect he or she offers to and receives from teammates.

- Pastors, rabbis, ministers who can write on leadership skills displayed by the applicant in his or her service to the church.

- School officials, such as guidance counselors, who have known an applicant through formative high school years and can comment on the maturity and ability of the applicant.

- Current math and English teachers who can attest to the applicant's attitude, analytical skills, class behavior, and potential for success in a collegiate environment.

- Active duty or retired U.S. Military members who can attest to an applicant's promise as a junior officer. Due to the military experience, this letter of recommendation is unofficially considered more influential than many of the others. Board members respect what a fellow serviceman has to say about an applicant. They have been in the military and have seen the qualities that young officers must possess. If a veteran or an active duty service member acknowledges that an applicant is officer material, the selection board takes note of it.

10

TIPS FOR THE ESSAY

In most ROTC applications, you are only required to write one essay, or "personal statement." Writing the essay does not have to be a painful experience. Think of it as your opportunity to show the selection board what the SAT and GPA cannot. The essay is your chance to convince the reader that you are special and different from the truckload of other applicants. In many cases, essays carry more weight than other aspects of your application because the words come from you. Well-written essays can help compensate for moderate test scores or a mediocre GPA.

Having noted that the essay can be a very powerful tool in your application, this chapter will hopefully provide you with suggestions and ideas that can help you compose a powerful essay. These essays belong to actual applicants from past applications. Any suggestions or critiques of their essays simply highlight potential good and bad points to which a board member would be drawn. Board members read a lot of essays and they can spot a strong essay just as quickly as they can spot a weak one. Hopefully, these suggestions will help you develop an essay with strong components that will appeal to the board member reading it.

SIMPLE QUESTION, SIMPLE ANSWER

The ROTC application provides you with minimal space within which to write your essay. In some cases, they even tell you not to exceed a certain number of words. You should strictly adhere to this challenge to be brief. When you look at the application form, you may wonder how you will ever fit all that you want to say into the small space provided. The idea of condensing your life's past and future into a single page is a bit ridiculous. Focus on what's important. The small space will help you concentrate on the question at hand, thereby forcing you to keep things simple. Plan what you want to say in the essay and then compose a rough draft. Revise it as necessary and have your English teacher read it. Selection board members have a stack of applications on their desks, all with essays. If you make your essay memorable and concise, they will thank you for it.

However, just because your essay has to be short, doesn't mean that it has to be dull. Trimming down your writing should provide you with the opportunity to use the correct words. Some applicants feel that they need a thesaurus in order to use only big words. Try to avoid big, awkward words that you'd only find in a dictionary. Sometimes, the use of big words can count against you. Board members know when certain vocabulary doesn't fit with the rest of your writing. Your SAT score already proves that you can use big words, so you don't need to use them in your essay. Keep it simple; small words with big intentions.

WRITE WITH ENTHUSIASM

The board member reading your application will appreciate lively writing. The English language provides many ways to add subtle humor to your writing. If you have the chance to replace a mundane word like "station-wagon" with "grocery getter," then do it. The selection board members rarely read essays with flavor. If you can, and you feel comfortable with it, then be creative with your words. Just don't be wordy. However, humor can also backfire on you. Someone with an objective eye should evaluate any humor that you put in your essay. Ask how it comes across to him or her. If he or she hesitates, delete it and try something else. You don't need to make the selection board members fall out of their chairs laughing. Just make them smile, or think, "Wow, this candidate has done some amazing things, and he or she has a good personality, too." Use your best judgment. Ideally, you're striving to put a slice of the real you into the application.

BE HUMBLE

Writing about yourself is not easy. You don't want to appear conceited, but you need to convey the reasons why you are special. You must write confidently about what you've done and about what you hope to do. You can use it as an opportunity to address any imperfection you perceive in your application.

EXAMPLE

...while I realize that my test-taking abilities are not the strongest, I feel that my GPA indicates my academic aptitude. I am not comfortable with my SAT scores, I wish I could present higher ones to the selection board. What I can present to you is the fact that one of my only dreams in life is to become an officer in the U.S. Army. What my SAT scores cannot account for in terms of my future success as an officer, perhaps my proven leadership both on and off school grounds can.

In this case, the writer describes a perceived imperfection along with offering an explanation that may transcend that imperfection. Selection board members value candor; don't feel as though you can't acknowledge or explain what you think is a weak aspect of your application. In fact, the selection board members prefer to see you address any deficiencies in your application. It keeps them from assuming the worst. Often times, a strong explanation is good enough for the board.

EDIT UNTIL IT'S RIGHT

When you've completed writing the essay's first draft, print it, and start revising it. Once you think it is decent, take it to a friendly critic, such as an English teacher. Tell him or her what the essay is for, who will be reading it, and ask for an honest opinion. Any corrections will only help you in the long run.

Once you've finished editing the essay and are ready to write it on the actual application, take this advice: make sure your handwriting is legible. After a board member reads fifty to one hundred essays, the thought of reading another (often illegible) essay is not an attractive prospect. Occasionally, after reading a number of chicken-scratch looking essays, a board member will encounter an applicant who took the time to slow down his or her handwriting for the sake of legibility. Imagine the sigh of relief from the board member reading it. Finally, a break in decoding! Some applications insist that the personal statements be handwritten. There is no reason to stray from the instructions. However, if the application does not provide enough space for your response, and there is no comment on the use of typing, feel free to present your essay in a typed format. It certainly makes the presentation of the essay more professional.

As a word to the wise, try to have at least one extra application in case you make a horrible mistake that white-out can't fix. There is nothing more unprofessional than a scholarship application covered with smudged ink and flakes of white-out. As a dry run, try photocopying your application and filling out the copy first. Then, when you are certain that all of your responses are good enough to be final, begin to work on the original.

COMMON ESSAY QUESTIONS, EXAMPLES AND ANALYSIS

WHY DO YOU WANT TO BE PART OF ROTC?

This type of question is among the most common found in ROTC scholarship applications. The selection boards use this question to assess your direction and level of commitment. They're also interested in seeing the degree to which you've thought about the ROTC program and about their particular service. Use this opportunity to show that your reasons for wanting to join the ROTC program are solid, and based on strong experiences. Don't tell them that it's your "dream" to be in the military and then not explain why. That information is worthless to the board member who wants to see the real you. Ensure that after reading your essay, the selection board knows that their particular service is a perfect match for you because of your specific goals. Match your qualities and strengths to the needs of the given branch of service. Applicants can, and often do, have the same GPA and SAT/ACT scores, but they will never have the same reasons for wanting to be a part of the U.S. Military. It's this reason that differentiates you from the countless other applicants with identical qualifications.

A good example of this type of question is from the 1998 U.S. NROTC application:

Example one

Please describe why you want to be an officer in the U.S. Military. How do you feel that your experiences to date have made you a good candidate?

Memorial Day, 1989, I was seven. My father and I went to see our town's parade. We joined the tail of the parade and followed it to its conclusion in the town's cemetery. I can remember only bits and pieces of the day: how sunny it was, the big American flag rustling in the breeze, the soldiers in their camouflage uniforms. The soldiers fired their rifles and then several fighters flew overhead. I can remember being struck by the honor that was being associated with the U.S. Armed Services, and that memory has never left me.

From that day on, I have known that I wanted to be a part of the U.S. Military. I want to be a part of an organization that is such a vital part of our nation, but more importantly, I want to be a part of the military. I feel that it will mold me into the type of person I have always admired, a strong leader. I have had leadership roles before. Sports, church group, and my job all gave me the chance to be a leader. I have a good background of experience with all my activities, but I am missing something. I feel that it is logical for me to join the military. For me, it's the next step in becoming the person I want to be.

So, I put forth considerable effort to make sure the military is for me. I have visited a local Naval Air Station and taken tours. I have read almost every book in my school library on the Navy. But most importantly I've spoken with a ROTC unit at my brother's college. Now I'm certain this program is for me, just as I did that Memorial Day in 1989.

This essay has a good approach. The beginning is interesting and attention-grabbing. The childhood memory is a nice touch because it shows the applicant's level of commitment. It's obvious that the notion of being in the military occurred to him as a child. This essay also portrays the sincerity of the candidate in his approach to the military. The applicant successfully links the beginning of his essay with the ending.

Example two

Consider carefully and then state below in the space provided why you wish to enroll in the Army ROTC program. Indicate in your statement how you believe your own objectives in life are related to the education and training offered by the Army ROTC and what career obligation means to you.

In today's advancing world, the demand for skilled leaders is increasing every day. The college graduate, however, has become commonplace and as a result, people who desire jobs face stiff competition. To gain a competitive edge, one must stand out either by knowledge or experience, and employers recognize this fact. I want to be different, and I will do anything for the competitive edge. For this reason, I feel that Army ROTC is the right choice for me. The skills, values, and experiences in ROTC are unique and highly valued by employers, as well as the Army.

I attended ROTC outings with my school's unit, in

hopes that I could show the Army that I was serious about my commitment and desire to become a part of it. From my first day in the program, I noticed a similarity in each senior cadet. It was only after more military exposure that I could identify that similarity; it was that they each had the honor, trust, and dedication of an officer. These qualities are what drive people to become their best and to succeed. I want those same qualities developed in me. Only after that development can I consider myself different, more competitive and the type of person I've always wanted to be. I am familiar with the type of education and training Army ROTC programs offer and I believe there is a good match here. The Army needs officers willing to lead by example and I am eager to transform into someone like that.

In the one semester that I have been a part of ROTC here at my school, I have learned a lot about the way the Army functions. Each day that I get up to exercise, I do so, not because I have to, but because I want to. I believe in fulfilling obligations and can describe completing the ROTC program as well as honorable service to the Army as "career obligation." I will make this obligation. I want this scholarship badly. I want to have the same pride that I've seen in the seniors of my unit. Without hesitation, I can say that I firmly believe in all that ROTC and being an officer stands for. It is these two things that actually inspire me to become an officer myself.

While it's written from a different point of view, this essay shows the applicant's high level of dedication. In this case, the applicant is already a freshman at a college with an ROTC unit. Having missed the chance to apply in high school, he is applying from a different vantage point. He has already trained with his school's ROTC unit, knows firsthand what it's like, and has displayed a high level of commitment.

The only troublesome point of this essay is the applicant's appearance as an individual who will serve only the minimum tour of duty required and then join the "workplace." While you might plan on joining the workplace, it's not the right thing to reveal to a selection board who is about to invest a lot of money in you. Notice how they specifically ask for your definition of "career obligation." Give them the impression that you want to make a career out of the military. Even if you are unsure about the military as a career, you have to look at it logically. You won't know if you want it as a career until you enter the program. So, get in to the military and then decide. You may end up really liking the military as many people do.

Essays on ethical dilemmas

For most applicants, writing a short essay on ethical dilemmas is a difficult task. First of all, what exactly qualifies as an "ethical dilemma?" Even after you answer the first question, you might spend countless hours trying to remember a situation that applies. For the purposes of the ROTC application, the ethical dilemma can be defined as a situation in which your moral beliefs were tested.

You may not have encountered an ethically questionable situation during the past three years of high school and, even if you can think of something, it probably doesn't seem very interesting. Try to recall a specific situation in which military values were tested and then elaborate on how you proved your mettle. It's a perfect opportunity for you to show the selection board that you have the qualities of a future military officer.

Example three

The Navy's core values are Honor, Courage, and Commitment. Please discuss a situation where you demonstrated one or more of these qualities and why that value is important to you.

During my junior year, several of my friends on the soccer team decided to vandalize the playing field of a rival high school. Although I found out about their actions after they had done it, our school officials quickly accused members of our team for the vandalism. Immediately, the team was brought in and questioned, but only a few people, including myself knew who the students were. At first I thought I could remain silent and that the whole thing would go away, but as I began to learn that the entire team would face disciplinary charges if the responsible members didn't come forward, I began to change my mind. I'm not a snitch; in fact, I'm very loyal to my friends. But what they were asking me and the rest of the team to do wasn't fair. I confronted one of my closer friends that were responsible at his house and I managed to convince him that he should come forward. Eventually, he did. I feel that I displayed a certain level of courage by confronting my friends. I value loyalty between friends, but I also value the courage it takes to stand up for what you believe in.

This essay is brief and cuts straight to the applicant's dilemma. Should he tell on his teammates or remain silent and face the team punishment? The important thing to remember is that the selection board is not looking to see if you are a Dudley Do-Right. They only want to confirm that you can recognize and act appropriately when you encounter an ethical dilemma. Just be brief; state the dilemma and then explain how you dealt with it.

YOUR GREATEST ACCOMPLISHMENT

This type of question can also be found in ROTC applications. Recently, it appeared in the 1999 Navy/Marine ROTC application. Essentially, this question attempts to uncover a few pieces of information that the application will invariably miss. If there is an experience or an accolade that has been pivotal in your life thus far, then here is the place to boast about it. Furthermore, it is also a good opportunity for the selection board to understand what you perceive as important. You can paint a more balanced picture of "you the applicant." For example, if every accomplishment you've noted in your application is sports-related, your life may appear unbalanced. Remember that military officers have to not only handle, but also control, many different operations at the same time. Clearly state why certain accomplishments are important to you. Don't be shy about marketing yourself, as the interview and the personal statement may be your only opportunities to do so.

Example four

What do you feel has been your greatest accomplishment to date? (NROTC)

As part of my passage to become an Eagle Scout, I had to determine a final project for myself. As a result of my love for reading and my love for building things, I decided to renovate a room at a local old folks home and build a library. I consider myself a handy person, but I had no idea what I was getting myself into when I started. Although the room was only 20' x 20' the project was big. I put in hard wood floors, made fourteen bookshelves which covered every inch of wall space, sanded and stained everything from top to bottom. And just when I thought I had reached the end, I realized that a person could never properly use this library without a card catalog system. So, with an old 486 computer (and the help of a friend), I built a database which assigned a call number to each title in the library's holdings (eight hundred books). The library was a smash hit at the home. I go by there all the time with my scout troop and now that there's some nice comfortable chairs in there, the staff there says that it's the most popular room by far. I'm so proud of it that I almost thought of enclosing pictures with this application. It was something that I built from nothing, and not many people can say that.

This essay does a good job of portraying the motivation and discipline of the applicant. The writer uses the essay to show a side of himself that the selection board would not have seen in any other part of the application. The applicant displays important officer-like qualities, such as attention to detail and the ability to successfully manage an ongoing project. Finally, the pride that the applicant expresses in his completed project indicates an individual who enjoys helping others—a trait that everybody should possess.

Why do you want to become an officer?

This type of question seeks to ensure that you are aware of the qualities that an officer must possess in order to succeed in the military. As it was mentioned earlier in the book, those qualities can generally be defined as honor, courage, commitment, loyalty, trust, leadership, honesty, and discipline. It's up to you to portray yourself as someone who has these qualities. The essay is your opportunity to suggest how perfect your qualities match those of the particular service.

Example five

Discuss your reasons for wanting to become an officer. (NROTC)

During my summers, I work as a coach at a local summer lacrosse camp. As a senior staff member of this camp, I have found myself in the position where I'm delegating my responsibilities for training the kids to other, subordinate staff members. It has been through this position that I have come to realize what an ideal proving ground this has been for me in terms of preparation for the military. First, I'm a stickler about leading by example. I want to make sure that if I tell my staff to have the kids run two laps around the field, that I'm the one leading the front. Through this position, I have also developed a strong sense of commitment. If I tell my staff to explain to all of the kids' parents that they can drop off their kids at 9:00 am, then my staff and I are here at 8:30 am. I have also learned how to discipline kids and get them motivated to do things the right way, eventually making them into better players. I want to become an officer because I like the qualities I've developed and the type of person that I've become. I want to continue this development and I feel that the Navy is the ideal place.

This essay conveys the applicant's understanding of which qualities are important in an officer. From the position of a coach, the applicant has already begun to develop a firsthand experience with leadership and accountability. Although this activity may have appeared in the application as merely a check in the community service box, it has become a very important part in the applicant's desire to become an officer. He successfully conveys that significance.

The 1999 Air Force ROTC scholarship application contains an essay question, which virtually echoes the above question, and is something that all selection boards want to know (i.e., "Why the military, and why an officer?"). Again, the way to approach this question is to consider the qualities that are required by an officer in any service. Then, demonstrate that (1) you have these qualities and (2) that because you have them, you feel that you would be a strong officer and, consequently, a good match for their particular service.

Example six

State briefly why you desire to receive a commission as an officer or pursue a military career. (AFROTC)

When I look at all the people around me in my (small) town, I can only recognize a few people that I could honestly say I admire. It wasn't too long ago when I realized that most of those people had served in the military. I began to ask a few of them about their military experiences. My neighbor, Mr. Pratt served in the Air Force for a short while in his early years. His qualities of leadership and confidence have always been impressive to me, and he is quick to point out that those were skills that the military helped him develop. Although I have shown some of these qualities in my extracurricular activities, I want to further develop them, and I would like the opportunity to do that in the Air Force.

In addition to pursuing a military career, I would also like the opportunity to attend college. It is my plan to participate in ROTC throughout college and accept a commission in the Air Force. I feel that because of my interest in math, I could possibly serve the military in that respect. From talking with recruiters and reading USAF ROTC brochures, I have learned that there are a lot of technical fields where my math skills could be used. Ultimately, though, the job I'm assigned isn't as important to me as the fact that I am afforded the chance to become an officer in the Air Force. It means much more to me to develop the qualities in myself that I admire so much in some of my neighbors, like Mr. Pratt.

This essay suggests that the applicant has a strong desire to not only become an officer, but a community leader, as well. His association between "admirable" members of the community and military service is a mature one, and perhaps indicative of an ability to eventually become a community leader himself. The applicant also clearly demonstrates his research of Air Force careers.

Another similar question that has recently appeared in the 1999 Navy/Marine ROTC application pertains to the factors that have influenced you in your quest for an ROTC scholarship. Although this question is similar to the preceding question (Why do you want to become an officer?) it's different in the respect that the selection board is looking specifically for what motivates you. Is it your family, friends, or a certain experience? When answered, this type of a question reveals a lot about an applicant. Many different things motivate people, and the selection board wants to ensure that your motivations have a strong foundation. Consider this short example:

Example seven

Explain your greatest influence in applying for an NROTC scholarship.

> When I was thirteen, my father took me up for the first time in his single engine Cessna. Since then, I have flown with him at least once every other month, not to mention the fact that I have nearly finished my requirements for my private pilot's license. Although my father was never in the military, he has been the greatest influence in my application for an ROTC scholarship. He has taught me so much about aviation, navigation and basic aerodynamics that I find myself feeling more comfortable traveling in a plane than I do in a car. I have wanted to be a pilot in the military ever since I saw my first air show four years ago. My desire to be a naval aviator has been a combination of my love for flying and a desire to use this skill to serve my country.

This applicant takes his inspiration from his father and from his love for flying. He conveys his interest in aviation as well as in the military. Although the essay is too short to probe further into the applicant's influences, it's clear that he has a sincere interest in both aviation and in the military.

What not to do in the essay

Below are some common mistakes that applicants make in their essays either because they aren't thinking clearly or because they don't care whether they're accepted or not.

- Don't start your essay by restating the question; it puts you at zero on the creativity scale.

- If you want to be a pilot, don't talk about the movie "Top Gun."

- Don't be afraid to mention the branch of service in your essay (i.e., Army, Navy, etc.). Without a reference to the specific service, the essay can have the appearance of a blanket essay which applicants use for several different ROTC applications.

- If you feel the need to mention your patriotism, do not make the claim that this quality makes you different. Unfortunately, it makes you the same as almost everybody else. Your patriotism is assumed, so focus on something else.

- If you run out of things to say, don't reiterate what you've already said or what the selection board can read in your application. Say something that they would never know about you–something from your heart that indicates your level of sincerity.

11

RECOMMENDATIONS

Every application requires that a minimum of three, and usually four, recommendations be filled out by specific people: a math teacher, an English teacher, and another school official of your choice. The selection board takes these letters of recommendation very seriously. The importance of choosing the appropriate people to write these recommendations cannot be overemphasized. Be very careful in who you choose. They must know you and like you well enough to sing your praises as a future officer. Don't pick the most popular English teacher just because you think he or she will write the best recommendation. Pick the English teacher who really knows you the best. If you feel comfortable, tell them what you feel the selection board looks for in an applicant and on which of your qualities they should focus.

WHO SHOULD WRITE RECOMMENDATIONS FOR YOU?

- Teachers/Officials who have known you for more than one year.

- People who have known you for more than five years.

- People who can testify to your desire to be in the military.

- People who can convey a good verbal picture of your character, integrity, and leadership ability.

• Retired or reserve members of the branch for which you are applying, who can testify that "having been in the USAF for twenty years, I only wish that I had a Lieutenant like Johnny under my command."

WHO SHOULD NOT WRITE RECOMMENDATIONS FOR YOU?

Bigwigs: They do not impress the board and, more often than not, they can hurt you more than they can help you. There are exceptions to this rule (e.g., if the individual knows you very well), but it's much more impressive to have a neighbor or coach who has known you for years applaud your leadership abilities.

People who can't write well: Pick someone whom you know has the ability to write well and can understand what guidance the board is seeking from him or her. It doesn't help your cause when someone who knows you extremely well has trouble spelling "leedership" [sic].

Teachers who could even remotely have the urge to describe you as less than a well-behaved student, or someone who will "eventually mature."
If you get to decide who writes the recommendations, why would you choose anyone that doesn't like or respect you? Choose wisely.

A BRIEF NOTE FROM YOU

Along with your application, it's always a nice touch to send along a well-written, typed note to the selection board that describes the people who are recommending you. The following is an example of such a note:

I have asked four people to write recommendations for me. Each of these people knows me in a different capacity, and has a unique perspective on my abilities. The first of these is Mrs. Stephanie Wilcox, my junior year English teacher. Mrs. Wilcox has been a huge influence on my writing abilities and has transformed me into a confident writer. The second is Mr. Dan Jaworski, my math teacher for two years. Mr. Jaworski can attest to my analytical ability. I spent two years studying under him and because of him have come to consider math my strongest subject. The third is Mr. Mike Lennon. Mr. Lennon has been my guidance counselor for the past three years of high school. In addition to being an advisor to me, Mr. Lennon is also a retired Major in the U.S. Marine Corps. He is a mentor and a friend whose advice has been invaluable. I hope you will find their comments helpful, but in case you have any questions, please feel free to give them a call.

Sincerely,
John Smith

If you are going to include additional recommendations, it's a good idea to provide an explanation. If the application asks for four letters, then provide four. Any more or less than it asks for looks suspicious. The selection board begins to ask, "Why is this applicant trying to overcompensate? Did we miss something in his application that makes him deficient in some way?" Then, they look for some deficiency. At this point, you're in trouble, because they'll always find one.

As a word to the wise: if you want to include a letter similar to the one above, feel free to do so, but do not copy this example word for word. This book is popular, and many applicants will have read it. It would not reflect well upon your integrity if your letter contained the same words as several other applicants. It's not hard to describe the unique views that these people can each offer as to your character, so just use your best judgment.

12

INTERVIEWS

This chapter provides background information to prepare you for your interviews. It also offers some recommendations on how you can use the interviews to your advantage. Understanding the role that the interview plays in this entire process is very important. If you have made it as far as the interview, you are a competitive applicant. The reason you have been scheduled for an interview is to further differentiate you from the rest of the applicants who have the exact same scores as you do. In this chapter, you will also be exposed to the most frequently asked questions about the interview process.

THE INTERVIEW IN A NUTSHELL

A local recruiter or ROTC official generally conducts the interview. It only lasts a total of about thirty to sixty minutes, but its role is critical because it gives the selection board a glimpse of the person behind the application. The interview is mandatory, as it is an element the selection board needs in order to make a scholarship decision. Think of it as your chance to present your goals to the selection board face to face. Do whatever you can to make the interviewer like you, because if your application is strong, but not a definite winner, the interview can push you closer to a scholarship.

As mentioned before, the interviewer will be an active duty military recruiter of the particular branch to which you are applying. If it's the Army, Marines, or the Air Force, the officer's rank will likely be that of a Captain. If it's the Navy, then a Lieutenant will most likely interview you. All interviewers are different. Some of the officers enjoy conducting the interviews, while some of them hate it. Don't worry about your interviewer because you have no control over him. You only have control over yourself and the image you project, so concentrate on that. When you interview with the recruiter, it will most likely occur in his office at the ROTC unit or at the recruiting station. Call and set up an appointment well ahead of time, as recruiters are busy people. If at all possible, write your application essay before the interview, as it will help you focus your thoughts on why you want to be in this particular branch of service. You may even want to bring it along for the interviewer to read. It could offer him greater insight about your ROTC aspirations.

BRING A RECOMMENDATION

Before you attend your application interview with the ROTC officer, make sure that you have a copy of your strongest letter of recommendation. This letter could be from a high school coach, an employer, a neighbor, or a family friend. However, the most important element to this letter of recommendation is that you have someone write it who thinks highly of you, and who can effectively convey the qualities that he or she likes about you.

When the conversation begins, the interviewer knows nothing about the real you. Everything he begins to understand about you will come from what you tell him. If you answer his questions and the interview ends after thirty minutes, then his impression of you is limited to the things he was able to learn in that time frame. Now, if you bring in a letter of recommendation from someone who can clearly identify your strongest qualities, effectively pointing them out to the interviewer, then the ROTC officer is no longer at ground zero. In fact, he starts off looking to confirm the qualities that the letter suggests are present in you.

An even better way to maximize the effect of this letter of recommendation is to find a former military serviceman or woman who can relate your qualities to potential success in the military. It's even better if you can have the letter addressed directly to the ROTC officer who is interviewing you. You would have to find out exactly which officer will be conducting your interview that day.

BRING A RÉSUMÉ

Try to put together a résumé of your accomplishments at school, as well as any employment history, or community involvement you might have had. Your parents, a high school guidance counselor, or a church elder are ideal people to approach for help in creating a résumé. By bringing a copy of your résumé, the interviewing officer will have a point by point resource to guide his discussion and questions. You can now anticipate what topics he will be curious about and you can prepare answers.

Frequently asked questions about the interview

Q: How is the interviewer going to affect my chances for winning a scholarship?
A: The interviewer is a virtual physical extension of the scholarship selection board. He is (1) an active military

person, and (2) very familiar with most scholarship applicants. Thus, his opinion is extremely valuable to the selection board. When the interviewer writes an evaluation of you and what you had to say, that recommendation is considered as good as gold.

Q: Is my interviewer given any guidelines by his military branch as to what topics to cover?

A: No, not usually. The interviewer's evaluation of the applicant must answer several questions for the selection board, and he can cover whatever topics he chooses as long as he can accurately answer those questions. Essentially, he must provide the selection board with a picture of the person behind the application. He asks questions that any employer would ask (e.g., "Tell me about yourself, etc..."). He can ask anything, as long as he can accurately answer questions about the applicant's appearance, determination, character, intellectual ability, personality, and future success as an officer.

Q: What should I wear for the interview?

A: The best way to approach the interview is to treat it like a job interview. Dress appropriately and there is usually nothing more to it. Don't come to his office in a ripped Ozzy Ozborne T-shirt and jeans, because that shows no respect for him, his time, or the ROTC program. ROTC is an officer program and officers lead by example. Men: wear an ironed button-down shirt with a tie, ironed trousers, and appropriate shoes. Women: wear either a nice dress or a blouse and dress pants. If applicants can dress appropriately, they're already ahead of a quarter of the applicants that these officers will interview.

Q: Is there any way to prepare for the interview?

A: Again, treat it like a job interview. Prepare to answer some basic questions about yourself and about what you know about the ROTC program. The interviewer will only ask you questions about yourself, so you should have a clear idea about specific ambitions and goals. Many applicants struggle through questions like, "Why are you interested in the ROTC program?" This answer should be the one they are prepared to give. The bottom line is that applicants should practice answering questions about themselves and about their goals.

Q: How can an applicant impress a military interviewer?

A: Ask Questions—intelligent questions. If you are interested in naval aviation, research the newest programs or the latest planes. Show some genuine, intelligent curiosity in a particular area of military interest. The applicants who usually do the best in the interviews are the ones who do their homework and prepare for the interview. The applicant who can effectively answer questions about what he wants out of the military and school will certainly impress the interviewer.

Q: Are there any topics that I should try to avoid in the interview?

A: Steer clear of any topic you cannot discuss with some level of clarity. In other words, try to minimize the "ahs" and "ums" in your conversations. Also, avoid discussing any recent news that could be potentially embarrassing to the military (i.e., aviation accidents, mishaps, or scandals).

Prepare for the Interview?

Fewer than twenty-percent of ROTC scholarship applicants prepare for the interview. It seems odd that the interview is the applicant's only chance to prove, in person, how much he or she wants a scholarship, and yet so few applicants prepare for it. Nevertheless, it's common for applicants to walk into the interview and give the impression that they have no idea what they want to do. If you think about it, this interview is just as important as any college interview, because (in many cases) if you don't win the scholarship, you can't afford to go to college. One has priority over the other. Be prepared for it.

But how do I prepare?

To begin, review everything that you have done in high school. All your activities, academics, and accomplishments are fair game to discuss. Be ready to ask the interviewer questions about current topics in the military. Find out in advance the recruiter's Military Occupational Specialty (MOS). Go to the library and scan some periodicals for current military issues pertaining to the recruiter's MOS. Asking him questions about his MOS will flatter him and make him feel more at ease during the interview. Believe it or not, interviews can often be uncomfortable for both parties involved.

As part of the preparation, you may want to run through some practice interviews. If you can find someone who is willing to play the role, have him or her ask you some routine questions like:

Tell me about yourself.
What do you do after school?
Give three words that best describe you.

Why are you interested in the military?
What will you study in college?
What would you like to do after the military?

You would be surprised at how much better your responses become after you have practiced them a few times. You will build your confidence to a level where you can supply a coherent answer to just about any question he asks you. If nothing else, it will help you to hear yourself answering these questions out loud.

When you begin the interview, you have sufficient ground to cover. There are several areas on which an interviewer will grade you. If he hasn't seen any evidence of your determination to be in the ROTC program by the end of the hour, then he makes an educated guess based upon your mutual discussion. That might hurt you. You may have more determination than all the other applicants put together, but if you don't show it or tell him of it, you might as well have no determination. Don't feel as though you have to sit back and let the recruiter lead you along the path he wants you to take. You only have an hour, so if you have the opportunity, tell him how serious you are about this scholarship. Use key words in your answers like integrity, determination, and leadership.

It's important that these interviews are a dialogue and not the Spanish Inquisition. If you feel the need and/or see the opportunity, gently turn the conversation to where you need it to go in order to cover what you feel are your strengths. However, make sure that you do not dominate the session. The interviewer has questions and topics that he needs to cover and you need to let him do that. Ideally, the interview should be a conversation, an open exchange of information, ideas, and opinions. You'll both enjoy the interview a lot more if it's a conversation, so don't be passive.

ACTUAL INTERVIEW QUESTIONS

Tell me about yourself, what sort of things are you interested in?

Why are you interested in the ROTC program?

Do you have a particular area of interest in the military? An MOS?

What do you know about this service's ROTC program?

What have you done that you are proud of?

What groups were you involved with in high school and what did you do in them?

What community service work have you done lately?

What leadership roles have you had?

Do you feel that your high school grades are reflective of your ability? Why or why not?

What do you want to study in college?

What specific questions do you have about the ROTC program?

WHAT NOT TO SAY

Here are some helpful hints as to what not to say during the interview:

"I only want the scholarship. The fact that I'll be in the military is secondary."

"Yes, I'm applying for every type of scholarship, but I really would like to be in the other branch."

"Um, I dunno." (In response to a question like, "What do you like to do in your spare time?" Or, "Tell me about yourself.")

"Yeah." (In response to any question)

"I like guns...big guns."

"I liked the movie 'Top Gun' a lot, and I think being in the military might be cool. "

Give the interviewer your full attention and try to seem interested in what he says. When you meet the recruiter, give a firm handshake, and address him by his title, "Afternoon Captain Smith, how are you, Sir?" Make sure that you sit up straight and don't make yourself comfortable until you are told to do so. Military etiquette is more formal than regular everyday etiquette. If you show the slightest bit of disrespect, the interviewer will crush you on his evaluation.

FOLLOW UP

After the interview, send the recruiter a quick thank-you note. It's a nice way to complete your interview process. It's also another way to get your name in front of the recruiter. You will most likely be the only applicant to send the interviewer a thank-you note. Often the interviewer is delayed in sending his interview results to the selection board. How beneficial would it be for you if he received your thank-you note before he ranked you among the rest of his applicants? You would probably rank at the top.

ONE LAST NOTE

These interviewers are the eyes and ears of the board. Barring any major discrepancies, the selection board always sides with the interviewer's recommendation. If the interviewer says that he likes you and he ranks you among the top of the applicants that he has interviewed, you have a great chance of winning a scholarship. In contrast, if the interviewer is not committed to you and to your place within the service, you will have a difficult time winning a scholarship. The members of the selection board are no different than the recruiters interviewing you and they know it. For that reason, they consider the opinions of the recruiter to be synonymous with an opinion that they themselves would render. The bottom line is to impress the interviewer because he will pave your way to a scholarship.

13

WHAT HAPPENS WHEN YOU SEND IN YOUR APPLICATION?

Applicants often assume that the scholarship selection board members are the first people to open the application envelopes. The truth is that your application arrives in the mailroom of some big military base and is sent directly to a pre-screening committee. This committee is usually comprised of two to three people who are only interested in qualifying you for the selection process. (This committee is not impressed if you send your application by overnight mail, so don't waste the money unless it's close to the application deadline). They take your application out of its envelope, throw the envelope away, and then place it in a plain manila folder.

This committee looks over the application to make sure that all the necessary qualifications have been met. Minimum GPA and SAT/ACT requirements are double-checked as well as other prerequisites. If these requirements are not met, or if you have any missing material, you are notified. It is in your best interest to make copies of everything you send to the selection board. It's rare, but sometimes a vital piece of your application can be lost in the shuffle. You can minimize this potential problem by having copies of everything you send to the selection board.

Don't wait until the last minute to mail your application. If there is something missing or incomplete within the application, you won't have time to re-submit it before the deadline. Your application will never make it to the selection board and will subsequently have to wait for the next time they convene. It should be noted that a surprising amount of applications are returned to the applicant because of a missing birth certificate, a missing recommendation, or a late high school transcript. Once the committee verifies that your application is complete, the application is then considered a "package." The package then waits for the selection board to convene. The wait may be anywhere from two weeks to two months depending on the branch of service.

When the board members walk into the boardroom for the first time, they see a stack of applications on their desks. From this point on, they consider these stacks to be their "populations." The members will read each package carefully, making notes and highlighting critical tidbits of information that shed light on the individual.

SHOULD I SEND ADDITIONAL MATERIAL TO THE BOARD?

Unless they ask for it, don't send it. Occasionally, a few applicants feel that their chances will improve if they send in copies of all the awards that they have ever received, including certificates from fourth grade spelling bees. These documents just add unnecessary time to the review process and, frankly, they don't tell the board anything important. If an applicant sends in additional, unsolicited material that advertises his or her assets, then the board assumes that the applicant is covering something up. The board will then take an even closer look at the applicant in question, carefully scrutinizing the application until they feel comfortable with a decision. The bottom line is that it's not a good idea to submit materials that aren't requested. If you feel as though you must share with the board members the many additional awards that you were not able to indicate on the application, then include an additional sheet of paper. The selection board will appreciate this brief summary much more than the actual award certificates.

14

HOW IS A BOARD
MEMBER SELECTED?

Applicants seem to think that scholarship selection boards are formed under a shroud of mystery, and that this mystery extends to the board members themselves. Understanding the background of the selection board is important to your success. It's difficult to write an appealing essay when you don't know who will be reading it. Since certain types of essays appeal to certain types of people, it is in your best interest to correctly aim your essay at the reader. In order to understand what type of people sit on the board, you must understand how they are selected. Who are these people, and how are they chosen for this selection board? This chapter will answer these questions and provide you with a clear understanding of the person reading your application.

Most of the selection boards convene on major military bases. They draw board members from military service personnel on that base. The board members are all U.S. Military officers who range in age and experience. Normally, they are officers from various occupational fields, such as infantry, logistics, administration, communications, armor, engineering, or aviation. They are temporarily assigned to this additional duty and, after it is completed, they return to their regular fields. Each service has its own board and, usually, members will serve on a board for one to three weeks. The three to fifteen members who are assigned to ROTC selection boards serve only in a temporary capacity. The number of board members ranges in size depending on the number of applications they handle per session. Air Force selection boards have a smaller number of applications because they convene regularly throughout the school year, while the Marine Corps selection board has considerably more applications because it only convenes twice a year. The larger services (i.e., the Army, Navy, and Air Force) receive such an incredible amount of applications throughout the year, that they often hold selection boards on a monthly basis. In this case, board members may hold a position for one day a month. However, generally the duration of an officer's assignment to a scholarship selection board is a few weeks.

Each branch of the U.S. military requires a certain number of board members each year. Usually, a memo circulates requesting one officer from each major department. This circulation ensures that the population of the board will represent a cross-section of that particular branch of service. For example, the Navy/Marine Option selection board requests ten members, each of whom have some background in every occupational field. This diversity renders a group that effectively represents the entire service. The president of the selection board is usually a senior-ranking officer who has served on the board several times. He or she is very familiar with the procedures and guidelines set forth by the particular service and ensures that the selection board abides by those guidelines.

Generally, these selection board members are experienced military officers who know what characteristics to look for in applicants. They can recognize good potential in an applicant because many of them went through an ROTC program.

Most importantly, these board members know which qualities will succeed in the military and which will fail.

Relax

You have no control over who reads your application. You can be sure that an active duty officer, who personally knows what it takes to succeed in the military, will read it. Show him or her that you have the necessary qualities that will enable you to succeed. It's important for you to know that the selection board is made up of people, not robots. The board member reading your application may become inspired or personally identify with some of your experiences and, as a result, go to bat for you. The most important thing to consider is that this board is comprised of people, just like you, who have a profound respect for this country. It's helpful to try to find a common denominator with them.

15

IN FRONT OF THE BOARD

As mentioned before, the board members walk into the boardroom for the first time and see a stack of applications on their desks. Your "briefer" is the board member who will review your individual application and subsequently make a recommendation to the board. However, before he gives his recommendation to the board, he must "brief" your package to the rest of the board. This briefing is a form of quality checking to make sure that someone doesn't recommend a poor candidate. Briefing is fairly simple and it takes about five to ten minutes per application. Basically, your briefer has read through your application, along with the many others he is briefing, and he ranks you against his other packages. If you fall at the top of the rankings, then he will brief your application among the first. Before he briefs your application, he goes through it with a highlighter, marking certain phrases out of your essay or comments written about you in a recommendation. He extracts pieces and forms a synopsis of your application to present to the board.

The Air Force, on the other hand, has a slightly different process. Again, they separate applicants into groups depending on intended majors. For example, all Electrical Engineers are evaluated together. Each major is assigned three board members, and each of those board members reads your application once and individually evaluates you. Once each board member has evaluated all of the applicants in a particular major, they then look at the applicants and examine the scores assigned to them by each of the other board members. If these scores vary significantly, they then re-evaluate the applicant in order to achieve a consensus. If you are applying for an AFROTC scholarship, this briefing process applies to you only in the sense that you will begin to understand how your reviewers take apart your application to get at the core elements.

BRIEFING YOUR PACKAGE

The selection board member who personally reads your application is called your "briefer." Your briefer spends anywhere from forty-five to sixty minutes reading your application. He or she reads the entire application, making a few notes here and there. Then, your briefer re-reads your application with a highlighter in hand, noting certain things said about you or key phrases that you wrote in your essay. An application can be very easy to brief or it can be dreadfully boring to brief. You have to picture your briefer standing up in the boardroom speaking on your behalf. He skims through your application and comments on the highlights he has made. If you have no major accomplishments or no real determination, your package is that much harder to pitch to his fellow board members.

Your briefer makes a sales pitch to the other board members. You want to make it easy for him to sell you. How do you do that? Give him proof that this scholarship is something that you really want. Either prove it in your interview or write it out in your essay. You want to make your application stand out from the others. If you would do anything to win an ROTC scholarship, then say that! Hold no enthusiasm back. Board members love to read applications with fervor, and they want to give these scholarships to applicants who have determination. They don't want to award them to the undecided and aimless. Rarely do applicants come across with an "I will do anything for this scholarship" or an "I've got to win this scholarship" type of attitude. Yet, this enthusiasm is precisely the sentiment you need to convey.

One of the most lighthearted moments of a normally mundane board is when a briefer reads a comment made by an applicant in his or her personal statement that makes them laugh. If you can make these people understand what is important to you and make them smile at the same time, they'll vote for you (That is, of course, assuming that what you said was intended to make them laugh).

How you're briefed

Here are some fictitious examples of briefs similar to those performed at a Navy ROTC Marine Option selection board.

"John Q Smith, from College Park, MD, GPA: 3.6 out of 4.0, SAT: 1250, Class rank: top 20%, Extracurricular activities: Student Gov't three years, class officer two of those years, President of Spanish club, Eagle Scout, Varsity Soccer and Track three years— two varsity letters, Member of church youth group. Notable comments from his essay: phrases like "ever since I can remember, I've wanted to be in the military" and "I have done some research on my own and traveled to several military bases in my area, [...] I believe that with my Eagle Scout background and love of the outdoors I would be an excellent infantry officer." Comments in letters of recommendation: "As John's Scoutmaster, I can honestly say that it is rare these days that I see a young man with as much motivation, determination and leadership ability." And, "as John's math teacher, I believe he is one of my brightest students and he will no doubt excel in any analytical environment." My opinion of this

applicant is a favorable one. He has obviously done his homework on our branch of the service, he has proven leadership ability, and has the prerequisite scores for a scholarship. My recommendation to the board is favorable."

"Susan Jones, from Great Falls, MT. GPA: 3.2 out of 4.0, SAT: 1100, Class rank: upper half, Extracurricular activities: Track and field captain, one varsity letter, head waitress at her family's restaurant, very active at church. Notable comments from her essay: "I realize that my grades are not what they should be, but I work 6 days a week to help support my family" and "Last summer I went to a nearby AFB for an air show. I was very impressed and knew right away that I wanted to become the first female U.S. Marine fighter pilot." Comments in letters of recommendation: "I am Susan's employer, but I am also her father. I can say from a business standpoint that I could not adequately run the restaurant without her management skills. In twenty years of the restaurant business, I have yet to come across a young lady that can command the respect of co-workers who are often five to ten years her senior. I realize that I am her father and a certain level of bias goes along with that role. However, I objectively assure you that she is strong, determined and, one hell of a people manager. She will not let you down." And, "as Susan's English teacher, I can say that she is a good student that does exceptional work. I understand that there is a need for her to work after school to support her family, and believe that if this were not the case you would be looking at a straight A student." My opinion of this applicant is a favorable one. She faces hardships uncommon to most applicants, but has met them with an admirable level of maturity. She has proven leadership/management ability, and while her scores are low I believe they would be otherwise if she had not had the obligation of helping the family business. My recommendation to the board is a favorable one."

LAYOUT OF THE ROOM

The layout of the boardroom varies between services as a result of the different number of members assigned to the board. As an applicant, it's good to have some idea about how the process works. Although understanding the layout of a boardroom isn't critical to the success of your application, the knowledge can provide a certain level of comfort for you during a normally mysterious application process. If you can picture your application moving through the various stages of the selection process, then you can spend less time worrying about at which stage your application is, and more time on the college admissions process.

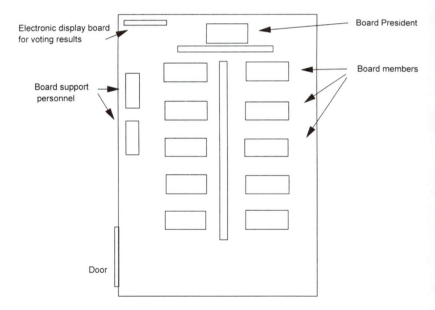

The diagram above is the floor layout of a Naval ROTC/ Marine Option boardroom. It's rectangular in shape and contains desks for the board members. At the front of the room is the president of the board. Although the other services may have slightly different boardrooms, the purpose is the same: brief applicants and share opinions. During the voting sessions, the doors are locked and the room is closed to anyone not associated with the board.

Voting process

After your package is briefed and a recommendation is given to the board, the board president asks if there are any questions about your particular application. If questions do arise, they usually focus on factors that don't make sense within your application. For example, the fact that you have straight A's, but a low SAT/ACT score. A board member might say, "Sounds like a strong applicant. What was his SAT score again? Really? Does the applicant offer any explanation for his low score?" The briefer might then respond, "Yes, the applicant noted that the night before he took the test, his mother was in a car accident, resulting in him taking the exam with little sleep. He attached a copy of the accident report in order to substantiate his claim." After the board addresses all questions about your application, the board president then calls for a vote. The Navy/USMC ROTC Option board conducts the vote through a private electronic voting system in which no member can know how another member votes. The votes are automatically tallied and displayed on an electronic display board at the front of the room. If there are eleven board members, including the president of the board, a vote of 11-0 would mean that all eleven members voted to give you a scholarship. The voting results of the board will range anywhere between a favorable 11-0 to an extremely unfavorable 0-11.

After the voting session is complete, the applications are grouped together, defined by the voting tallies, and the scholarships are assigned. First, all the applicants who received 11-0 votes would win a scholarship. If, after that, there were three hundred scholarships remaining, the applicants who received 10-1 votes would earn scholarships. If, after that, there were two hundred scholarships remaining, then scholarships would be awarded to all the 9-2 votes. The process continues until there are no more scholarships to award. There is a finite number of scholarships and once they're gone, that's it until the next meeting of the board.

The Army, Navy, and Air Force hold selection boards throughout the year on a regular basis. The reason is because of the sheer volume of applications they receive. Due to its smaller size, the Marine Corps offers roughly a quarter of the number of scholarships offered by the other services. Consequently, it only holds two boards throughout the year, fall and spring. Much like the college admissions process, the earlier you apply in a given academic year, the better your chances of receiving a scholarship. If your application is received in time for the convening of the first selection board, and for some reason you are not selected, your application will automatically be entered for the next round of selections. Conceivably, your application could receive two or three shots at a scholarship in one year. Those are some pretty good odds. Find out the first deadline for your particular service and make sure the application is completed on time. For most services, the first deadline is sometime in late fall, such as November.

THE POINT SYSTEM

All the military services differ in their methods of applicant selection, but one element remains the same: each service must rank the applicants against one another. They have to develop a system that facilitates this process. More often than not, the board ranks applicants by the use of a point system. Understanding this point system could be the key to maximizing your chances of winning a scholarship. The ROTC scholarship applications are basically Scantron sheets (fill in the appropriate circles with a number two pencil). While these are a pain for applicants, they make the job of data entry extremely simple for the selection boards. Your application is sent through the Scantron reader and a computer stores all of your information. Once it's digitized, this information becomes easier to handle. More importantly, it becomes easier for applicants to be compared with one another.

The board members separate the packages into groups through a point scoring system. As the reviewing officer examines each application, points are awarded for certain accolades. An applicant's GPA can generate anywhere from one to three points, and the same applies to the SAT/ACT scores and class rank. Extracurricular activities are considered in the same manner. Depending on if you play multiple sports, were a team captain, or were involved in five different school clubs, you could be assigned one to nine points. Although they are outside of school, community activities count for just as much. Boy/Girl/Eagle Scout, church youth group, martial arts, or any type of community membership, could bring you one to seven points. Personal awards, both academic and community, can bring one to three points. The personal statement, if exceptional, can add a point or two at the board member's discretion. The number of points you have when the member is finished examining your package determines where in the selection process your package is briefed.

The number of points your application generates is key to your survival. If your application generates more than the average number of points (let's say fifteen), then you will be one of the first packages to be briefed. Why is the order of briefing important? Remember that there is only a certain number of scholarships available for the board to offer. A package has a better chance of being accepted at the beginning of the briefing process as opposed to later, because there are less slots available as the voting proceeds. It becomes highly competitive.

What if you were more involved in community activities and spent more of your free time outside of school rather than in? That is perfectly acceptable. Make sure that (1) the importance of the activity is highlighted, (2) your achievements in it are adequately noted, and (3) how it differentiates you from the next applicant is emphasized. Knowing that your application is graded on a point system offers a big advantage to anyone applying for a scholarship. Now, you have that advantage.

16

RESULTS OF THE BOARD

Once the decision is final, the results are tabulated, cross checked and double-checked to make sure that the approved applicants have met all of the prerequisites set by the board. A formal and compiled list of the scholarship winners is then presented to the selection board. Each board member must approve the results and then sign the bottom of the document. The approved list is then circulated to the appropriate department, which notifies all scholarship winners. The time required for the list's approval can take anywhere from two to four weeks. After that period, the letters of acceptance and/ or deferral are sent out a week later. The turnaround time for most of the services is usually about four to six weeks.

ACCEPTED

If you receive a letter awarding you an ROTC scholarship, there are a few things you should do. First, celebrate! You have made a huge accomplishment and deserve to enjoy the fact that your distinctions have helped you survive a highly competitive selection process. Second, you still must gain admission into a college or university where you can utilize the ROTC scholarship. Often times, this part is more difficult than winning the scholarship. Third, you must contact your local ROTC selection officer. He or she will need to confirm your acceptance as well as give you information about your scholarship.Assuming that you are admitted to a college or university that offers your specific ROTC program, it will send you a packet of information detailing where and when you are required to report to school. Normally, ROTC students are required to arrive a week or two early for orientation purposes.

Denied

If you receive a letter denying you a scholarship, do not beat yourself up about it. More than likely, you were competing with an applicant pool that had well above average scores. This situation will happen from time to time, but you shouldn't let it dissuade you from continuing your pursuit of an ROTC scholarship. There are other ways to win these scholarships and, in many cases (depending on the branch of service), there are three or more ROTC scholarship programs that you can apply for once you're at college.

Understandably, it's disappointing to be one of the applicants who is not selected, but you have to remember that you are part of the majority. Selection rates for most four-year ROTC scholarships hover around twenty to twenty-five percent. Scholarship selection rates for most two and three-year programs are much higher at around forty-percent. It's much easier to obtain a scholarship once you're at the school and involved in the ROTC unit. So, don't be too hard on yourself. Keep your determination to be a member of ROTC and an officer in the U.S. military, and you will achieve your goal.

Alternate list

If you receive a letter indicating that you were selected as an alternate for a four-year ROTC scholarship, you may not know what to feel. On one hand, you weren't denied the scholarship, but, on the other hand, you weren't offered one either. Have patience and cross your fingers. The alternate list means that the selection board decided that you merit a scholarship, but due to a limited supply, it is unable to offer you one unless a certain number of recipients decide to defer theirs. In this case, you would then be offered the newly-available scholarship.

When students are awarded a scholarship, they have a time frame of a few weeks (after notification) wherein they must either accept or defer the scholarship. Once this two to three-week period expires, the various ROTC programs have a fairly clear idea as to how many scholarships they now have available to offer to their list of alternates. Being on the alternate list is an uncomfortable situation. First, you have a painful three to four weeks of waiting until you hear whether or not you've been offered a scholarship. Second, you still have to gain admission to a college or university with your particular ROTC program in case you are awarded the scholarship.

Overall, it's not so bad to be on the alternate list. Things can, and many times do, work out for the better. For instance, it's not uncommon for stellar applicants to receive ROTC scholarship offers from more than one branch of service. They can only choose one and, as a result, the scholarships they defer are offered to students on the alternate list. The alternate list is put together in a structured format wherein the students whose applications receive the highest scores from the selection board are placed at the top, and the other alternate applicants are arranged in descending order. As the scholarships become available, students on the alternate list are notified in the order that they appear on the list.

APPENDIX A

ROTC Scholarship
Application Checklist

Carefully read your application. Some parts of it are to be completed by you, while other parts are to be completed by your high school officials. The following checklist is provided to assist you in reviewing your application for general completeness. It cannot possibly include every detail which may pertain to your specific application. It's up to you (not your guidance counselor or ROTC recruiter) to make sure that *all* of the application's requirements are met in a timely fashion.

- ❏ All required sections are promptly completed and signed by you.

- ❏ If necessary, these sections are immediately passed on to school official for signature.

- ❏ Prepare and take the SAT or ACT.

- ❏ SAT/ACT scores must be officially sent to ROTC selection board (see code inside application).

- ❏ High school transcript information – signed by school office.

- ❏ Contemplate potential people to write the letters of recommendation (math teachers, English teachers, etc.).

❑ English instructor recommendation –
signed by evaluator.

❑ Math instructor recommendation – signed by
evaluator.

❑ Other recommendation(s) – signed by evaluator(s).

❑ Applicant's personal statement – signed by you.

❑ Ensure all correspondence not attached to initial
application forms include your Social Security
Number and home address/phone.

❑ Perforated cards, if included, must be completed
and included with application (postage not required).

❑ Prepare for and schedule ROTC interview.

❑ Schedule an ROTC unit or military base visit.

APPENDIX B

Service numbers for ROTC issues

US Army
1 (800) USA-ROTC
Website: www-rotc.monroe.army.mil/

US Air Force
1 (334) 953- and the appropriate extension listed below.
If your last name begins with___Dial extension___

A-Cl	2592	L-N	2849
Cm-Go	2820	O-Sl	4383
Gr-K	4382	Sm-Z	4380
No Answer:	778	Fax:	4384

Website: www.afoats.af.mil/rotc.htm/

US Navy
1 (800) USA NAVY
Website: www.cnet.navy.mil/nrotc/nrotc.htm

US Marines
NROTC applications include Marine Corps scholarships.
Questions that relate specifically may be directed to:

1 (800) MARINES
Website: www.cnet.navy.mil/nrotc/nrotc.htm

APPENDIX C

**LIST OF COLLEGES
WITH ROTC PROGRAMS**

NAVY ROTC PROGRAMS

(N) indicates a nursing program is available

ALABAMA
Auburn University (N), (334) 844-4364

ARIZONA
University of Arizona (N), (520) 621-1281,
Cross Town Affiliate: Pima Community College

CALIFORNIA
University of California at Berkeley (N), (510) 642-3551, *Cross Town Affiliates*: California Maritime Academy, Stanford University, University of California at Davis, University of California at Los Angeles (N), (310) 825-9075, University of San Diego (N), (619) 260-4600, *Cross Town Affiliates*: San Diego State University, University of Southern California (N), (213) 740-2663

COLORADO
University of Colorado (N), (888) 600-6289, *Cross Town Affiliates*: University of Colorado at Denver, University of Colorado Health Sciences Center (N)

DISTRICT OF COLUMBIA
George Washington University (N), (202) 994-9107, *Cross Town Affiliates*: Georgetown University, Howard University, The Catholic University of America (N), University of Maryland at College Park

FLORIDA
Florida A&M University (N), (850) 599-3980, *Cross Town Affiliates*: Florida State University, Tallahassee Community College, Jacksonville University (N), (904) 745-7480, *Cross Town Affiliates*: Florida Community College at Jacksonville, University of North Florida,

University of Florida (N), (352) 392-0973

GEORGIA

Georgia Institute of Technology (N), (404) 894-4771,
Cross Town Affiliates: Southern College of Technology, Georgia State
University, Morehouse College (N), (404) 756-9561, *Cross Town
Affiliates*: Clark Atlanta University, Morris Brown College, Spelman
College, Savannah State University (N), (912) 356-2206,
Cross Town Affiliate: Armstrong Atlantic University

IDAHO

University of Idaho (N), (208) 885-6333, *Cross Town Affiliates*:
Intercollegiate Center for Nursing Education (N), Lewis-Clark State
College (N), Washington State University

ILLINOIS

Illinois Institute of Technology (N), (312) 567-3530, *Cross Town
Affiliate*: University of Illinois at Chicago, Northwestern University
(N), (847) 491-3324, *Cross Town Affiliate*: Loyola University, University
of Illinois (N), (217) 333-1061, *Cross Town Affiliate*: Parkland College

INDIANA

Purdue University (N), (765) 494-2055, University of Notre Dame
(N), (219) 863-7274, *Cross Town Affiliates*: Indiana University at
South Bend (N), St. Mary's College

IOWA

Iowa State University, (515) 294-6050

KANSAS

University of Kansas (N), (785) 864-3161,
Cross Town Affiliates: Baker University (N), Washburn University

LOUISIANA

Southern University and A&M College (N), (225) 771-4370, *Cross
Town Affiliate*: Louisiana State University, Tulane University (N),
(504) 865-5104, *Cross Town Affiliates*: Dillard University, Loyola
University, Xavier University

MAINE

Maine Maritime Academy (N), (800) 227-8465, *Cross Town Affiliates*:

Husson College (N), University of Maine at Orono
MASSACHUSETTS
Boston University (N), (617) 353-0471, *Cross Town Affiliates*: Boston College (N), Northeastern University (N), College of the Holy Cross (N), (508) 793-2433, *Cross Town Affiliates*: Worcester Polytechnic Institute (N), Worcester State College (N), Massachusetts Institute of Technology, (617) 253-2991, *Cross Town Affiliates*: Harvard University (N), Tufts University (N)

MICHIGAN
University of Michigan (N), (734) 764-1498,
Cross Town Affiliate: Eastern Michigan University

MINNESOTA
University of Minnesota (N), (612) 625-6677, *Cross Town Affiliates*: Macalester College (N), University of Saint Thomas (N)

MISSISSIPPI
University of Mississippi, (662) 915-5831

MISSOURI
University of Missouri (N), (573) 882-6693,
Cross Town Affiliate: Columbia College (N)

NEBRASKA
University of Nebraska (N), (402) 472-2475

NEW MEXICO
University of New Mexico (N), (505) 277-3744

NEW YORK
Cornell University, (607) 255-5604, Rensselaer Polytechnic Institute (N), (518) 276-6251, *Cross Town Affiliates*: Russell Sage College (N), Union College (N), University of Rochester (N), (716) 275-4275, *Cross Town Affiliates*: State University of New York Maritime College at Brockport, Rochester Institute of Technology, State University of New York Maritime College (N), (718) 409-7231,
Cross Town Affiliates: Fordham University (N), Molloy College (N)
NORTH CAROLINA
Duke University, (919) 660-3700, North Carolina State University,

(919) 515-6317, University of North Carolina (N), (919) 962-1198

OHIO

Miami University (N), (513) 529-3700, Ohio State University (N), (614) 292-6015

OKLAHOMA

University of Oklahoma (N), (405) 325-2021

OREGON

Oregon State University, (541) 737-6289

PENNSYLVANIA

Carnegie Mellon University (N), (412) 268-5109, *Cross Town Affiliate*: University of Pittsburgh (N), Pennsylvania State University (N), (814) 865-7452, University of Pennsylvania (N), (215) 898-7436, *Cross Town Affiliates*: Drexel University (N), Temple University (N), Villanova University (N)

SOUTH CAROLINA

The Citadel (N), (843) 953-5176, *Cross Town Affiliate*: The Medical University of South Carolina (N), University of South Carolina (N), (803) 777-4124

TENNESSEE

University of Memphis (N), (901) 678-2370, Vanderbilt University (N), (615) 322-2671, *Cross Town Affiliates*: Belmont University (N), Tennessee State University (N)

TEXAS

Prairie View A&M University (N), (409) 857-2310, Rice University, (713) 527-4825, *Cross Town Affiliates*: Houston Baptist University (N), University of Houston, Texas A&M University, (409) 845-1775, *Cross Town Affiliate*: Texas A&M University at Galveston, University of Texas (N), (512) 471-7649

UTAH

University of Utah (N), (801) 581-6723,
Cross Town Affiliates: Weber State University, Westminster College

VERMONT

Norwich University (N), (802) 485-2185

Virginia

Hampton University (N), (757) 727-5720, Norfolk State University (N), (757) 823-8895, Old Dominion University (N), (757) 683-4684, Virginia Military Institute, (540) 464-7275,

Cross Town Affiliate: Mary Baldwin College, Virginia Polytechnic Institute (N), (540) 231-7883, *Cross Town Affiliate*: Radford University (N), University of Virginia (N), (804) 924-0970

Washington

University of Washington (N), (206) 543-0170

Wisconsin

Marquette University (N), (414) 288-7076, University of Wisconsin (N), (608) 262-3794

ARMY ROTC PROGRAMS

ALABAMA

Alabama A&M University (001002) (205) 851-5775

Auburn University (001009) (205) 844-4305

Auburn University at Montgomery (008310) (205) 244-3528

Jacksonville State University (001020) (205) 782-5601

Marion Military Institute (001026) (334) 683-2327

Tuskegee University (001051) (334) 727-8370

University of Alabama (001051) (205) 348-5917

University of North Alabama (001016) (205) 760-4271

University of South Alabama (001057) (334) 460-6341

University of Alabama–Birmingham (001052) (205) 934-7215

Students at the following cross-enrolled schools may also take Army ROTC classes at UAB (for more information, contact the Military Science Department at UAB using the number above):

Birmingham Southern College (001012) • University of Montevallo (001004) • Miles College (001028) • Samford University (001036)

ALASKA

University of Alaska–Fairbanks (001063) (907) 474-7501

ARIZONA

University of Arizona (001083) (520) 621-1078

Arizona State University (001081) (602) 965-3318

In addition, students at the following cross-enrolled schools may also take Army ROTC classes at Arizona State University:

Grand Canyon University (001074) • Phoenix College (001078) • Northern Arizona University (001082) (520) 774-5131

Students at Embry-Riddle Aeronautical University (029022) in Prescott

141

may also take ROTC classes at Northern Arizona through a cross-enrollment agreement. For details contact the NAU Department of Military Science at (520) 774-5131.

ARKANSAS

Arkansas State University (001090) (501) 972-2064

University of Arkansas (001108) (501) 575-4251

University of Arkansas–Pine Bluff (001086) (501) 543-8448

University of Central Arkansas (001092) (501) 450-3145

CALIFORNIA

California Polytechnic State Univ (001143) (805) 756-7682

California State Univ–Fresno (001147) (209) 278-2887

California State Univ–Fullerton (001137) (714) 773-3007

San Diego State University (001151) (619) 594-4943

Santa Clara University (001326) (408) 554-4781

Claremont-McKenna College (001170) (909) 624-7965

University of California–Berkeley (001312) (510) 642-3374

Students at the following cross-enrolled schools may also take Army ROTC classes through the University of California-Berkeley. For details, contact the Cal Department of Military Science at (510) 642-3374:

California State University, Hayward (001138) • Mills College (001238) • St. Mary's College (001302) • Samuel Merritt College (007012) • San Francisco State University (001154) • Sonoma State University (001156) • University of California–Davis (001313) (916) 752-5211• University of California–Los Angeles (001315) (310) 825-7381 • University of California–Santa Barbara (001320) (805) 893-2769 • University of San Francisco (001325) (415) 422-6405 • University of Southern California (001328) (213) 740-4026

In addition, students at California State University–Long Beach (001139) can take Army ROTC classes through a cross-enrollment agreement at the University of Southern California. For details, contact the USC Department of Military Science at (213) 740-4026, or the Long Beach Army ROTC office at (562) 985-5766.

Colorado

University of Colorado–Colorado Springs (004509) (719) 262-3520

Colorado State University (001350) (970) 491-6506

Cross-enrolled students at the University of Northern Colorado (001349) may also take Army ROTC courses at Colorado State. For details, contact the CSU Department of Military Science at (970) 491-6506.

University of Colorado–Boulder (001370) (303) 492-3549

In addition, students at the Colorado School of Mines (001348) may take Army ROTC classes through a cross-enrollment agreement at the University of Colorado–Boulder. For details, contact the Colorado Military Science Department at (303) 492-3549.

Connecticut

University of Connecticut (001417) (860) 486-4538

In addition, students at the following schools may take Army ROTC classes through a cross-enrollment agreement at the University of Connecticut. For details, contact the UConn Department of Military Science at (860) 486-4538:

Yale University (001426) • Eastern Connecticut State University (001425) • Central Connecticut State University (001378)

Southern Connecticut State University (001406)

Fairfield University (001385)

Quinnipiac College (001402)

Delaware

University of Delaware (001431) (302) 831-2217

District of Columbia

Howard University (001448) (202) 806-6784

Georgetown University (001445) (202) 687-7056

In addition, students at the following cross-enrolled schools may also take Army ROTC classes at Georgetown University. For details, contact the Georgetown Department of Military Science at (202) 687-7056:

American University (001434)

Marymount University (003724)

The Catholic University of America (001437)

The George Washington University (001444)

Trinity College (001460)

University of Maryland (002103)

University of the District of Columbia (001441)

FLORIDA

Embry-Riddle Aeronautical University (001479) (904) 226-6470

Florida A & M University (001480) (904) 599-3515

Florida Institute of Technology (001469) (407) 768-8000, ext. 8094

Florida International University (009635) (305) 348-1619)

Florida Southern College (001488) (941) 680-4240

Florida State University (001489) (904) 644-1016

The University of Tampa (001538) (813) 258-7200

University of Central Florida (003954) (407) 823-2430

University of Florida (001535) (352) 392-1395

University of South Florida (001537) (813) 974-4065

University of West Florida (003955) (904) 474-2198

GEORGIA

Georgia Military College (001571) (912) 454-2731

Georgia Southern University (001572) (912) 681-5320

Georgia State University (001574) (404) 651-2275

North Georgia College (001585) (706) 864-1776

University of Georgia (001598) (706) 542-2612

Augusta State University (001552) (706) 737-1643

Columbus State University (001561) (706) 568-2058

Fort Valley State University (001566) (912) 825-6340

In addition, students at Albany State University (001544) can take Army ROTC classes through a cross-enrollment agreement at Fort Valley State. For details, contact the Fort Valley State Department of Military Science at (912) 825-6340.

Georgia Institute of Technology (001569) (404) 894-4760

Students at the following cross-enrolled schools may also take Army ROTC classes through Georgia Tech. For details, contact the Georgia Tech

Military Science Department at (404) 894-4760:

Clark Atlanta University (001559)

Emory University (001564)

Kennesaw State University (001577)

Morehouse College (001582)

Morris Brown College (001583)

Southern Polytechnic State University (001570)

Spelman College (001594)

Hawaii

University of Hawaii (001610) (808) 956-7744

Idaho

Boise State University (001616) (208) 385-3500

University of Idaho (001626) (208) 885-6528

Illinois

Eastern Illinois University (001674) (217) 581-5944

Illinois State University (001692) (309) 438-5408

Northern Illinois University (001737) (815) 753-0574

Southern Illinois University (001758) (618) 453-5786

Southern Illinois University–Edwardsville (001759) (618) 692-2500

University of Illinois Champaign-Urbanna (001775) (217) 333-3418

In addition, students at Parkland College (007118) can take Army ROTC classes through a cross-enrollment agreement at the University of Illinois. For details, contact the University of Illinois Department of Military Science at (217) 333-3418.

University of Illinois–Chicago (001776) (312) 996-3451

In addition, students at the following cross-enrolled schools in the Chicago area may take Army ROTC classes at UIC. For details, contact the Military Science Department at UIC, (312) 996-3451: Chicago State University (001694) • DePaul University (001671) • Governor's State University (009145) • Illinois Institute of Technology (001691)

In addition, students at the following cross-enrolled schools in the Chicago area may take Army ROTC classes at IIT:

Indiana University Northwest (001815) • Loyola University

(001710) • Northeastern Illinois University (001693) • Northwestern University (001739) • Purdue University Calumet (001827) • Roosevelt University (001749) • St. Xavier University (001768) • Triton College (001773) • University of Chicago (001774) • Western Illinois University (001780) (309) 298-1161 • Wheaton College (001781) (630) 752-5121

In addition, students at the following cross-enrolled schools may take Army ROTC classes at Wheaton. For details contact the Military Science department at Wheaton College, (630) 752-5121:

Lewis University (001707) (815) 838-0500, ext. 5357

Olivet Nazarene University (001741) (815) 939-5011

DeVry Institute of Technology (001672)

Aurora University (001634)

North Central College (001734)

Northwood University (008759)

Judson College (001700)

Elmhurst College (001676)

College of St. Francis (001664)

College of DuPage (006656)

Rush University (009800)

INDIANA

Ball State University (001786) (317) 285-8343

Indiana University (001809) (812) 855-7682

Indiana U.–Purdue U. at Indianapolis (001813) (317) 274-2691

In addition, students at the following cross-enrolled schools can take Army ROTC classes at IUPUI. For details, contact IUPUI Department of Military Science at the number listed above:

Butler University (001788) – freshman and sophomore level classes are taught at Butler; junior and senior classes taught at IUPUI.

Indiana University Kokomo (001814)

University of Indianapolis (001804) – freshman and sophomore level classes are taught at U of I; junior and senior classes taught at IUPUI.

Marian College (001821) – classes are taught at IUPUI. • Franklin College (001798) – classes are taught at IUPUI.

Purdue University (001825) (317) 494-2099

Rose–Hulman Institute of Technology (001830) (800) 248-7448, ext. 8326

In addition, students at the following cross-enrolled schools can take Army ROTC classes at Rose-Hulman. For details, contact the Rose-Hulman Department of Military Science at (800) 248-7448, ext. 8326:

Indiana State University (009563)

DePauw University (001782)

St. Mary of the Woods College (001835)

Vincennes University (001843)

University of Notre Dame (001840) (800) UND-ARMY

In addition, students at the following cross-enrolled schools can take Army ROTC classes at Notre Dame. For details, contact the Notre Dame Department of Military Science at (800) UND-ARMY:

Holy Cross College (007263) • St. Mary's College (001836) • Indiana University at South Bend (001816)

Iowa

The University of Iowa (001892) (319) 335-9187

University of Northern Iowa (001890) (319) 273-6178

Iowa State University (001869) (515) 294-1852.

In addition, students at the following cross-enrolled schools may take Army ROTC classes at Iowa State University. For details, contact the Iowa State Department of Military Science at (515) 294-1852: • Drake University (001860). Call (515) 271-3898. • Grand View College (001867)

Kansas

Kansas State University (001928) (913) 532-6754

Pittsburg State University (001926) (316) 235-4859

University of Kansas (001948) (913) 864-3311

Kentucky

Eastern Kentucky University (001963) (606) 622-1205

Morehead State University (001976) (606) 783-2050
University of Kentucky (001989) (606) 257-2696
University of Louisville (001999) (502) 852-7902
Western Kentucky University (002002) (502) 745-4293

LOUISIANA

Grambling State University (002006) (318) 274-2646

In addition, students at the following cross-enrolled schools may take Army ROTC classes at Grambling State University. For details, contact the Grambling Department of Military Science at (318) 274-2646:

Louisiana Tech University (002008) • Northeast Louisiana University (002020) • Louisiana State University (0020100) (504) 388-2371

In addition, students at the following cross-enrolled schools can take Army ROTC classes at Louisiana State. For details, contact the LSU Department of Military Science at (800) 256-4578:

Southeastern Louisiana University (002024) • University of Southwestern Louisiana (002031) • Northwestern State University (002021) (318) 357-5156

In addition, students at the following cross-enrolled schools may take Army ROTC classes at Northwestern State University. For details, contact the Northwestern State Department of Military Science at (318) 357-5156 or 1-800-217-6045:

Centenary College (002003) • Louisiana State University-Shreveport (002013) • East Texas Baptist University (003564) • Southern University and A & M College (002025) (504) 771-4160 • Tulane University (002029) (504) 865-5594

In addition, students at the following cross-enrolled schools may take Army ROTC classes at Tulane University. For details, contact the Tulane Department of Military Science at (504) 865-5594:

Dillard University (002004) • Louisiana State University Medical Center (002014) • Loyola University (002016) • Our Lady of Holy Cross College (002023) • Southern University at New Orleans (002026) • University of New Orleans (002015) • Xavier University of Louisiana (002032)

MAINE

University of Maine (002053) (207) 581-1122

In addition, students at the following cross-enrolled schools may take Army ROTC classes at the University of Maine. For details, contact the University of Maine Department of Military Science at (207) 581-1122:
Colby College (002039) • Husson College (002043)

MARYLAND

Bowie State University (002062) (301) 464-6692

Loyola College (002078) (410) 617-2387

Morgan State University (002083) (410) 319-3263

The Johns Hopkins University (002077) (410) 516-7474

Western Maryland College (002109) (410) 876-3804

MASSACHUSETTS

Boston University (002130) (617) 353-4025

Massachusetts Institute of Technology (002178) (617) 494-8710

Northeastern University (002199) (617) 373-2372

In addition, students at the following cross-enrolled schools can take Army ROTC classes at Northeastern University. For details, contact the Northeastern Department of Military Science at (617) 373-2372: Boston College (002128)

Eastern Nazarene College (002145)

Emmanuel College (002147)

Framingham State College (002185)

Massachusetts College of Art (002180)

Salem State College (002188)

Simmons College (002208)

Suffolk University (002218)

University of Massachusetts-Boston (002222)

Wentworth Institute of Technology (002225)

University of Massachusetts (002221) (413) 545-2321

In addition, students at the following cross-enrolled schools can take Army ROTC classes at the University of Massachusetts. For details, contact the UMass Department of Military Science at (413) 545-2321:

American International College (002114) • College of Our Lady of the Elms (002140) • Mount Holyoke College (002192) • Smith College (002209) • Springfield College (002211) • Western New England College (002226) • Westfield State College (002189) Worcester Polytechnic Institute (002233) (508) 752-7209

In addition, students at the following cross-enrolled schools may take Army ROTC classes at Worcester Polytechnic. For details, contact the Worcester Department of Military Science at (508) 752-7209:
Assumption College (002118) • Atlantic Union College (002119) • Clark University (002139) • College of the Holy Cross (002141) • Fitchburg State College (002184) • Framingham State College (002185) • Nichols College (002197) • University of Massachusetts-Lowell (002161) • Worcester State College (002190)

MICHIGAN
Michigan State University (002290) (517) 355-1913
Michigan Technological University (002292) (906) 482-4481
Northern Michigan University (002301) (906) 227-2236
Central Michigan University (002243) (517) 774-3049
Eastern Michigan University (002259)

In addition, students at the University of Detroit Mercy (002323) can take Army ROTC classes at Eastern Michigan University through a cross-enrollment agreement. For details, contact the EMU Department of Military Science at (734) 487-1020.
University of Michigan (002325) (313) 764-2400

In addition, students at the following cross-enrolled schools can take Army ROTC classes at the University of Michigan. For details, contact the University of Michigan Department of Military Science at (313)764-2400:
University of Michigan-Dearborn (002326) • University of Michigan-Flint (002327) • Concordia College, Ann Arbor 002247)
Western Michigan University (002330) (800) WMU-ROTC

In addition, students at the following cross-enrolled schools can take Army ROTC classes at Western Michigan University. For details, contact the

Western Michigan Department of Military Science at (800) WMU-ROTC: Albion College (002235) • Aquinas College (002239) • Calvin College (002241) • Cornerstone College (002266) • Davenport College 002249) • Grand Valley State University (002268) • Hope College (002273) • Kalamazoo College (002275) • Olivet College (002308) • Southwestern Michigan College (002317)

MINNESOTA

Minnesota State University, Mankato (002360) (507) 389-6229

In addition, students at the following cross-enrolled schools may also take Army ROTC classes at Mankato State University. For details, contact the Mankato State Military Science Department at (507) 389-6229: • Bethany Lutheran College (002337) • *Gustavus Adolphus College (002353)* • *Saint John's University (002379) (320) 363-3827*

In addition, students at the following cross-enrolled schools may also take Army ROTC classes at St. John's University. For details, contact St. John's Military Science Department at (320) 363-3827: College of Saint Benedict (002341) • St. Cloud State University (002377) • University of Minnesota (003969) (612) 624-7300

In addition, students at the following cross-enrolled schools may also take Army ROTC classes at the University of Minnesota. For details, contact the University of Minnesota Military Science Department at (612) 624-7300: Augsburg College (002334) • Bethel College (009058) • College of St. Catherine (002342) • Concordia College (002347) • Macalester College (002358) • North Central Bible College (002369) • Northwestern College (002371) • University of St. Thomas (002345)

MISSOURI

University of Missouri–Rolla (002517) (573) 341-4744

Washington University (002520) (314) 935-5537

Wentworth Military Academy (002522) (816) 259-2219

Central Missouri State University (002454) (816) 543-4866

Kemper Military School and College (002475) (660) 882-5347

Lincoln University (002479) (573) 681-5346

Missouri Western State College (002490) (816) 271-0096

Southwest Missouri State University (002503) (417) 836-5791

Truman State University (002495)

University of Missouri (002516) (573) 882-7721

In addition, students at the following cross-enrolled schools may also take Army ROTC classes at the University of Missouri. For details, contact the Missouri Department of Military Science at (573) 882-7721:

Columbia College (002456) • Stephens College (002512) • Westminster College (002523) • William Woods University (002525)

MISSISSIPPI

Alcorn State University (002396) (601) 877-6370

Jackson State University (002410) (601) 968-2175

Mississippi State University (002423) (601) 325-3503

University of Mississippi (002440) (888) UMS-ARMY

University of Southern Mississippi (002441) (601) 266-4456

MONTANA

Montana State University (002532) (406) 994-4044

University of Montana (002536) (406) 243-2769

NEBRASKA

Creighton University (002542) (402) 280-2828

University of Nebraska (002565) (402) 472-2468

NEVADA

University of Nevada (002568) (702) 784-6751

NEW HAMPSHIRE

University of New Hampshire (002589) (603) 862-1078

NEW JERSEY

Rutgers University (006964) (908) 932-7328

Seton Hall University (002632) (201) 763-3078

Princeton University (002627) (609) 258-4225

In addition, students at the following cross-enrolled schools can take Army ROTC classes at Princeton University. For details, contact the Princeton Department of Military Science at (609) 258-4225:

College of New Jersey (002642) • Rider College (002628) • The

Richard Stockton College of New Jersey (009345)

NEW MEXICO

New Mexico Military Institute (002656) (505) 624-8296

New Mexico State University (002657) (505) 646-4030

NEW YORK

Hofstra University (002732) (516) 463-5648

Niagara University (002788) (716) 286-8230

Rochester Institute of Technology (002806) (716) 475-2881

Canisius College (002681) (716) 884-5811

Clarkson University (002699) (315) 265-2180

Cornell University (002711) (607) 255-4000

Fordham University (002722) (718) 817-4875

In addition, students at Polytechnic University (002796) may take Army ROTC classes through a cross-enrollment agreement at Fordham University. For details, contact the Fordham Department of Military Science at (718) 817-4875 or 1-800-NYC-ROTC

Siena College (002816) (518) 783-2536

In addition, students at the following cross-enrolled schools may take Army ROTC classes at Siena College. For details, contact the Siena College Military Science Department at (518) 783-2536:

Albany College of Pharmacy of Union University (002885) • Colgate University (002701) • College of Saint Rose (002705) • Marist College (002765) • Rennsselaer Polytechnic Institute (002803) • Russell Sage College (002810) • Skidmore College (002814) • State University of New York, Albany (002835) • State University of New York, New Paltz (002846) • State University of New York College of Agriculture and Technology, Cobleskill (002856) • State University of New York College of Technology, Delhi (002857) • State University of New York Empire State College (010286) • Union College (002889)

Saint Bonaventure University (002817) (716) 375-2508

In addition, students at the following cross-enrolled schools may take Army ROTC classes at St. Bonaventure University. For details, contact the St. Bonaventure Department of Military Science at (716) 375-2508:

Alfred University (002668) • Alfred State University (002854) •
Houghton College (002734) • University of Pittsburgh–Bradford (Pa.)
(003880) • St. John's University (002823) (718) 380-5582 • State
University of New York–Brockport (002841) (716) 395-2249
• Syracuse University (002882) (315) 443-2462

*In addition, students at the following cross-enrolled schools may take
Army ROTC classes at Syracuse University. For details, contact the
Syracuse Department of Military Science at (315) 443-2462:*
Cazenovia College (002685) • Colgate University (002701) •
Hamilton College (002728) • LeMoyne College (002748) • SUNY-
Oswego (002848) • SUNY College of Environmental Science and
Forestry (002851) • SUNY A & T- Morrisville (002859) • SUNY
Institute of Technology-Utica/Rome (011678) • Utica College
(002883)

NORTH CAROLINA

Appalachian State University (002906) (704) 262-2015
Campbell University (002913) (910) 893-1580/1-800-334-4111
Duke University (002920) (919) 660-3090

*In addition, students at North Carolina Central University (002950) can
take Army ROTC classes at Duke University through a cross-enrollment
agreement. For details, contact the Duke Department of Military Science at
(919) 660-3090.*
East Carolina University (002923) (919) 328-6967
Elizabeth City State University (002926) (919) 335-3237
North Carolina A & T State University (002905) (910) 334-7552
North Carolina State University (002972) (919) 515-2428
Saint Augustine's College (002968) (919) 832-4825
University of North Carolina–Chapel Hill (002974) (919) 962-5546/
1-800-305-6687
University of North Carolina–Charlotte (002975) (704) 547-2411

*In addition, students at the following cross-enrolled schools can take
Army ROTC classes at UNC-Charlotte. For details, contact the UNC-
Charlotte Department of Military Science at (704) 547-2411:*

Barber-Scotia College (002909) • Belmont Abbey College (002910) • Catawba College (002914) • Davidson College (002918) • Johnson C. Smith University (002936) • Lenoir-Rhyne College (002941) • Livingstone College (002942) • Pfeiffer University (002955) • Queens College (002957) • Wingate University (002985) • Winthrop University (003456)

Wake Forest University (002978) (910) 759-5308

In addition, students at the following cross-enrolled schools may take Army ROTC classes at Wake Forest. For details, contact the Wake Forest Department of Military Science at (910) 759-5308:

Winston-Salem State University (002986) • Salem College (002960)

North Dakota

North Dakota State University (009265) (701) 231-7575

University of North Dakota (003005) (701) 777-2259

Ohio

Bowling Green State University (003018) (419) 372-2476

Capital University (003023) (614) 236-7114

Central State University (003026) (513) 376-6279

John Caroll University (003050) (216) 397-4421

Kent State University (003051) (330) 672-2769

Ohio University (003100) (614) 593-1919

In addition, students at the University of Rio Grande (003116) may take Army ROTC classes through a cross-enrollment agreement at Ohio University. For details, contact the Ohio University Military Science Department at (614) 593-1919.

The Ohio State University (006883) (614) 292-6075

University of Akron (003123) (330) 972-7454

University of Cincinnati (003125) (513) 556-3660

University of Dayton (003127) (513) 229-3326

University of Toledo (003131) (419) 530-2681

Wright State University (003078) (513) 873-2763

Xavier University (003144) (513) 745-3646

Students at the following cross-enrolled schools may also take Army

ROTC classes at Xavier University. For details, contact the Xavier Department of Military Science at (513) 745-3646:
College of Mount St. Joseph (003033) • Miami University (007104) • Northern Kentucky University (009275) • Thomas More College (002001)

OKLAHOMA

Cameron University (003150) (513) 745-3646 (405) 581-2340
Oklahoma State University (003170) (405) 744-1775
University of Central Oklahoma (003152) (405) 341-2980, ext. 5005
University of Oklahoma (003184) (405) 325-3012

OREGON

Oregon State University (003210) (541) 737-3511
University of Oregon (003223) (541) 346-7682
University of Portland (003224) (503) 283-7353

PENNSYLVANIA

Bucknell University (003238) (717) 524-1246
In addition, students at the following colleges can take Army ROTC classes at Bucknell University through a cross-enrollment agreement. For details, contact the Bucknell Military Science Department at (717) 524-1246:
Bloomsburg University (003315) • Lycoming College (003293) • Pennsylvania College of Technology (003395) • Susquehanna University (003369) • Dickinson College (003253) (717) 245-1221
• Drexel University (003256) (215) 590-8808
In addition, students at the following cross-enrolled schools may take Army ROTC classes through Drexel University. For details, contact the Drexel Military Science Department at (215) 590-8808:
Gwynedd-Mercy College (003270) • LaSalle University (003287) • Philadelphia College of Pharmacy and Science (003353) • Rowan University (002609) • Rutgers University-Camden (004741) • St. Josephs's University (003367) • Thomas Jefferson University (003278) • University of Pennsylvania (003378) • Edinboro University of Pennsylvania (003321) (814) 732-2562 • Gannon University

(003266) (814) 871-7524

In addition, students at the following cross-enrolled schools can take Army ROTC classes at Gannon. For details, contact the Gannon Department of Military Science at (814) 871-7524:

Allegheny College (003230) • Mercyhurst College (003297) • Pennsylvania State University-Erie (003333) • Indiana University of Pennsylvania (003277) (412) 357-2700 • Lehigh University (003289) (610) 758-3275

In addition, students at the following cross-enrolled schools can take Army ROTC classes at Lehigh University. For details, contact the Lehigh Department of Military Science at (610)758-3275:

Albright College (003229) • Allentown College of St. Francis de Sales (003986) • Alvernia College (003233) • Cedar Crest College (003243) • Kutztown University (003322) • Moravian College (003301) • Muhlenberg College (003304) • Pennsylvania State University-Allentown (003330) • Lock Haven University of Pennsylvania (003323) (717) 893-2299 • Shippensburg University (003326) (717) 532-1782 • Slippery Rock University (003327) (412) 738-2019 • Temple University (003371) (215) 204-7480 • Valley Forge Military Academy and College (003386) (610) 687-9495 • Widener University (003313) (610) 499-4097 • The Pennsylvania State University (003329) (814) 863-0368

In addition, the Department of Military Science offers Army ROTC classes on the following Penn State campuses. For details, call (814) 863-0368:

Abington College (003342) • Altoona 003331) • Berks (003334) • Hazelton (003338) • University of Pittsburgh (003379) (412) 624-6197

In addition, students at the following cross-enrolled schools may take Army ROTC classes through the University of Pittsburgh. For details, contact the Pitt Department of Military Science at (412) 624-6197:

California University of Pennsylvania (003316) • Carlow College (003303) • Carnegie-Mellon University (003242) • Chatham College (003244) • Duquesne University (003258) • LaRoche College (003987) • Pennsylvania State University-New Kensington (003341)

• Point Park College (003357) • Robert Morris College (003359) •
Saint Vincent College (003368) • University of Pittsburgh-
Greensburg (003381) • Washington & Jefferson College (003389)
• University of Scranton (003384) (717) 941-7457

*In addition, students at the following cross-enrolled schools may also
take Army ROTC classes at the University of Scranton. For details,
contact the Scranton Department of Military Science at (717) 941-7457:*
Baptist Bible College (002670) • College Misericordia (003247) •
Keystone College (003280) • King's College (003282) • Marywood
College (003296) • Pennsylvania State University (Wilkes-Barre)
(003346) • Pennsylvania State University (Worthington) (003344) •
Wilkes University (003394)

SOUTH CAROLINA
Clemson University (003425) (864) 656-3107
Furman University (003434) (864) 294-2160
Presbyterian College (003445) (864) 833-8441
South Carolina State University (003446) (803) 536-7233
The Citadel (003423) (803) 953-5224
University of South Carolina (003448) (803) 777-6542
Wofford College (003457) (864) 585-7373

SOUTH DAKOTA
South Dakota School of Mines (003470) (605) 394-2769
South Dakota State University (003471) (605) 688-6151
University of South Dakota (003474) (605) 677-5284

TENNESSEE
Austin-Peay State University (003478) (615) 648-6155

*In addition, students at the following cross-enrolled schools can take
Army ROTC classes at Austin-Peay. For details, contact the Austin-Peay
Department of Military Science at (615) 648-6155:*
Embry-Riddle Aeronautical University, Fort Campbell (001479) •
Murray State University (001977) • Carson-Newman College
(003481) (423) 471-3374 • East Tennessee State University (003487)
(423) 439-4269 • Middle Tennessee State University (003510) (615)

898-2470 • Tennessee Tech University (003523) (615) 372-3283 • University of Memphis (003509) (901) 678-2933 • University of Tennessee (003530) (423) 974-5371 • University of Tennessee at Martin (003531) (901) 587-7151 • Vanderbilt University (003535) (615) 322-8550

In addition, students at the following cross-enrolled schools may also take Army ROTC classes at Vanderbilt. For details, contact the Vanderbilt Department of Military Science at (615) 322-8550:
American Baptist College (010460) • Belmont University (003479) • Fisk University (003490) • Free Will Baptist College (003491) • Lipscomb University (003486) • Tennessee State University (003522) • Trevacca Nazarene University (003526)

TEXAS
Prairie View A & M University (003630) (409) 857-4612
Saint Mary's University (003623) (210) 436-3415

In addition, students at the following cross-enrolled schools may take Army ROTC classes at St. Mary's University. For details contact the St. Mary's Department of Military Science at (210) 436-3415:
Our Lady of the Lake University (003598) • Palo Alto College (023413) • San Antonio College (009163) • St. Philip's College (003608) • University of the Incarnate Word (003578)
Sam Houston State University (003606) (409) 294-1306 • Southwest Texas State University (003615) (512) 245-3232 • Stephen F. Austin State University (003624) (409) 468-4505 • Tarleton State University (003631) (254) 968-9188 • Texas A & M University (010366) (409) 845-2814 • Texas A & M University–Kingsville (003639) (512) 593-3201 • Texas Christian University (003636) (817) 257-7455 • Texas Tech University (003644) (806) 742-2141 • University of Houston (003652) (713) 743-3875

In addition, students at the following cross-enrolled schools can take Army ROTC classes at the University of Houston. For details, contact the University of Houston Military Science Department at (713) 743-3875:
Houston Baptist University (003576) • Rice University (003604) •

Texas Southern University (003642) • Texas Women's University (003646) • University of Houston–Downtown (012826) • University of St. Thomas (003654) • University of Texas Health Science Center (011618)

University of Texas–El Paso (003661) (915) 747-5621 • University of Texas–Pan American (003599) (956) 381-3600 • University of Texas at San Antonio (010115) (210) 691-4622 • University of Texas at Arlington (003656) (817) 272-3281/2378 • University of Texas at Austin (003658) (512) 471-5919

In addition, students at the following cross-enrolled schools can take Army ROTC classes at the University of Texas-Austin. For details, contact the Military Science Department (512) 471-5919:

Concordia University at Austin (003557) • Huston-Tillotson College (003577) • St. Edward's University (003621) • University of Central Texas (011854)

UTAH

Brigham Young University (003670) (801) 378-7729/(800)872-2707, ext. 7729

University of Utah (003675) (801) 581-6716

Weber State University (003680) (801) 626-6518

In addition, students at Utah State University (003677) can take Army ROTC classes through a cross-enrollment agreement at Weber State University. For details, contact the Weber State Department of Military Science at (801) 626-6518.

VERMONT

Norwich University (003692) (802) 485-2480

University of Vermont (003696) (802) 860-4998

Students at the following cross-enrolled schools may also take Army ROTC classes at the University of Vermont. For details, contact the University of Vermont Military Science Department at (802) 860-4998:

Castleton State College (003683) • Champlain College (003684) • Johnson State College (003688) • Lyndon State College (003689) • Middlebury College (003691) • Saint Michael's College (003694) •

Southern Vermont College (003693) • Trinity College (003695)

VIRGINIA

George Mason University (003749) (703) 993-2706

Hampton University (003714) (757) 727-5244

James Madison University (003721) (540) 568-6264

Norfolk State University (003765) (757) 683-8541

Old Dominion University (003728) (757) 683-3663

The College of William and Mary (003705) (757) 221-3600

In addition, students at Christopher Newport University (003706) may take Army ROTC classes through a cross-enrollment agreement at The College of William and Mary. For details, contact the William and Mary Military Science Department at (757) 221-3600.

University of Richmond (003744) (804) 289-8540

In addition, students at the following cross-enrolled schools can take Army ROTC classes at the University of Richmond. For details, contact the Richmond Department of Military Science at (804) 289-8540:

Hampden-Sydney College (003713) • Longwood College (003719) • Randolph-Macon College (003733) • Virginia Commonwealth University (003735) • Virginia State University (003764) (804) 524-5216 • University of Virginia (003745) (804) 924-7101 • Virginia Military Institute (003753) (540) 464-7351 • Virginia Polytechnic Institute and State University (003754)
(540) 231-6401.

In addition, students at Radford University (003732) may take Army ROTC classes through a cross-enrollment agreement at Virginia Tech. For details, contact the Virginia Tech Military Science Dept. at (540) 231-6401.

WASHINGTON

University of Washington (003798) (206) 543-9010

Washington State University (003800) (509) 335-2591

Central Washington University (003771) (509) 963-3518

Eastern Washington University (003775) (509) 359-2386/6110

Gonzaga University (003778) (509) 328-4220, ext. 3116

Seattle University (003790) (206) 296-6430

Students at Pacific Lutheran University can take Army ROTC classes at Seattle University through a cross-enrollment agreement. For details, contact the Seattle University Department of Military Science at (206) 296-6430.

WEST VIRGINIA

Marshall University (003815) (304) 696-6450

West Virginia State College (003826) (304) 766-3109

West Virginia University (003827) (304) 293-2911

WISCONSIN

Marquette University (003863) (414) 288-7195

University of Wisconsin–La Crosse (003919) (608) 785-6760

In addition, students at the following cross-enrolled schools may take Army ROTC classes at the University of Wisconsin-LaCrosse. For details, call the Military Science Department at LaCrosse, (608) 785-6760:

Viterbo College (003391) • Winona State University (Winona, MN) (002394) • St. Mary's University (Winona, MN) (002380) • University of Wisconsin–Madison (003895) (608) 262-3411/9758

In addition, students at the University of Wisconsin-Whitewater (003926) may also take Army ROTC classes at Madison. For more details call Army ROTC at (414) 472-1541.

University of Wisconsin–Oshkosh (003920) (920) 424-3400

Students at the following cross-enrolled schools may take Army ROTC classes at UW-O. In addition, the University of Wisconsin-Oshkosh and these cross-enrolled schools offer special financial incentives to students taking Army ROTC courses:

Bellon College of Nursing (006639) (920) 337-1160. • Marian College (003861). (920) 923-8730. • Ripon College (003884) (920) 748-8168. • St. Norbert College (003892) (920) 337-1160. • University of Wisconsin-Green Bay (003899) (920) 337-1160. • University of Wisconsin–Stevens Point (003924) (715) 346-3821

WYOMING

University of Wyoming (003932) (307) 766-3390

AIR FORCE ROTC PROGRAMS

Det 005 Auburn University, Auburn (334)844-4355

Det 010 University of Alabama, Tuscalusa (205) 348-5900

Det 012 Samford University, Birmingham (205) 870-2621

Det 015 Tuskegee University, Tuskegee (334) 727-8388

Det 017 Troy State University, Troy (334) 670-3383

Det 019 Alabama State University, Montgomery (334)229-4304

Det 432A University of Southern Alabama, Mobile (334) 460-7211

ARIZONA

Det 020 University of Arizona, Tuscon (520) 621-3521

Det 025 Arizona State University, Tempe (602) 965-3181

Det 027 North Arizona University, Flagstaff (520) 523-2049

Det 028 Embry Riddle Aero. University, Prescott (520) 708-3868

ARKANSAS

Det 030 University of Arkansas, Fayetteville (501) 575-3651

CALIFORNIA

Det 085 University of California at Berkeley, Berkeley
(510) 642-3572

Det 035 California State University, Fresno (209) 287-2593

Det 060A Cal State University, San Bernadino (909) 880-5440

Det 055 UCLA, Los Angeles (310) 825-1742

Det 055A Loyola Marymount University, Los Angeles
(310) 338-2770

Det 088 Cal State Sacramento, Sacramento (916) 278-7315

Det 075 San Diego State, San Diego (619) 594-5545

Det 060 University of Southern California, Los Angeles
(213) 740-2670

Det 105 University of Colorado, Boulder (303) 492-8351

Det 090 Colorado State University, Fort Collins (970) 491-6476

Det 115 University of Connecticut, Storrs (860) 486-2224

Det 128 University of Delaware, Newark (302) 831-2863

Det 130 Howard University, Washington D.C. (202) 806-6788

Det 145 Florida State University, Tallahassee (850) 644-3461

Det 150 University of Florida, Gainsville (352) 392-1355

Det 155 University of Miami, Coral Gables (305) 284-2870

Det 157 Embry Riddle Aero University, Daytona Beach
(904) 226-6880

Det 158 University of South Florida, Tampa (813) 974-3367

Det 159 University of Central Florida, Orlando (407) 823-1247

GEORGIA

Det 160 University of Georgia, Athens (706) 542-1751

Det 165 Georgia Institute of Technology, Atlanta (404) 894-4175

Det 172 Valdosta State College, Valdosta (912) 333-5954

HAWAII

Det 175 University of Hawaii, Manoa, Honolulu (808) 956-7762

ILLINOIS

Det 190 University of Illinois, Champaign (217) 333-1927

Det 195 Illinois Institute of Technology, Chicago (312) 567-3525

Det 205 Southern Illinois University, Carbondale (618) 453-2481

INDIANA

Det 215 Indiana University, Bloomington (812) 855-4191

Det 218 Indiana State University, Terre Haute (812) 237-2657

Det 220 Purdue University, West Lafayette (765) 494-2042

Det 225 University of Notre Dame (219) 631-6634

IOWA

Det 250 Iowa State University, Ames (515) 294-1716

Det 255 University of Iowa, Iowa City (319) 335-9205

KANSAS

Det 270 Kansas State University, Manhattan (913) 532-6600

Det 280 University of Kansas, Lawrence (785) 864-4676

KENTUCKY

Det 290 University of Kentucky, Lexington (606) 257-7115

Det 295 University of Louisville, Louisville (502) 852-6576

LOUISIANA

Det 305 Louisiana Tech University, Ruston (318) 257-2740

Det 310 Louisiana State University A&M, Baton Rouge (504) 388-4407

Det 311 Grambling State University, Grambling (318) 274-2233

Det 320 Tulane University, New Orleans (504) 865-5394 ext 4

MARYLAND

Det 330 University of Maryland, College Park (301) 314-3242

MASSACHUSETTS

Det 340 Worcester Polytechnic University, Worcester (508) 831-5747

Det 345 University of Massachusetts, Lowell (978) 934-2252

Det 355 Boston University, Boston (617) 353-4705

Det 365 Massachusetts Institute of Technology, Cambridge (617) 253-4475

Det 370 University of Massachusetts, Amherst (413) 545-2451

MICHIGAN

Det 380 Michigan State University, East Lansing (517) 355-2168

Det 390 University of Michigan, Ann Arbor (313) 747-2404

Det 400 Michigan Technological University, Houghton (906) 487-2652

MINNESOTA

Det 410 University of Saint Thomas, St Paul (612) 962-6320

Det 415 University of Minnesota, Minneapolis (612) 625-2884

Det 420 University of Minnesota, Duluth (218) 726-8159

MISSISSIPPI

Det 425 Mississippi State University, Mississippi State (601) 325-3180

Det 430 University of Mississippi, University (601) 232-7058

Det 430a Mississippi Valley State University, Itta Bena (601) 254-3480

Det 432 University of Southern Mississippi, Hattiesburg (601) 266-4468

MISSOURI

Det 207 St. Louis University, St Louis (314) 977-8227

Det 440 University of Missouri, Columbia (314) 882-7621

Det 442 University of Missouri, Rolla (513) 341-4925

MONTANA

Det 450 Montana State University (406) 994-4022

NEBRASKA

Det 465 University of Nebraska, Lincoln (402) 472-2473

Det 470 University of Nebraska, Omaha (402) 554-2318

NEW HAMPSHIRE

Det 475 Univ of New Hampshire, Durham (603) 862-1480

NEW JERSEY

Det 485 Rutgers University, New Brunswick (908) 932-7430

Det 490 New Jersey Institute of Technology, Newark (973) 596-3626

NEW MEXICO

Det 505 New Mexico State University, Las Cruces (505) 646-2136

Det 510 University of New Mexico, Albuquerque (505) 277-4502

NEW YORK

Det 520 Cornell University, Ithica (607) 255-4004

Det 535 Syracuse University, Syracuse (315) 443-2461

Det 536 Clarkson University, Potsdam (315) 268-7989

Det 538 Rochester Institute of Technology, Rochester (716) 475-5196

Det 550 Rensselaer Polytechnic Institute, Troy (518) 276-6236

Det 560 Manhattan College, Riverdale (718) 862-7901

NORTH CAROLINA

Det 585 Duke University, Durham (919) 660-1860

Det 590 UNC-Chapel Hill, Chapel Hill (919) 962-2074

Det 592 UNC-Charlotte, Charlotte (704) 547-4537

Det 595 NC State University, Raleigh (919) 515-2417

Det 600 East Carolina University, Greenville (919) 328-6597

Det 605 NC A&T State University, Greensboro (910) 334-7707

Det 607 Fayetteville State University, Fayetteville (910) 486-1464

North Dakota

Det 610 North Dakota State University, Fargo (701) 231-8186

Ohio

Det 620 Bowling Green State University, Bowling Green (419) 372-2176

Det 630 Kent State University, Kent (330) 672-2182

Det 630a University of Akron, Akron (330) 972-7654

Det 640 Miami University, Oxford (513) 529-2031

Det 643 Wright State University, Dayton (973) 775-2730

Det 645 Ohio State University, Columbus (614) 292-5441

Det 650 Ohio University, Athens (614) 593-1343

Det 665 University of Cincinnati, Cincinnati (513) 556-2237

Oklahoma

Det 670 Oklahoma State University, Stillwater (405) 744-7744

Det 675 University of Oklahoma, Norman (405) 325-3211

Oregon

Det 685 Oregon State University, Corvallis (541) 737-3291

Det 695 University of Portland, Portland (503) 283-7216

Pennsylvania

Det 720 Pennsylvania State University, University Park (814) 865-5453

Det 730 University of Pittsburg, Pittsburg (412) 624-6396

Det 750 St. Joseph's University, Philadelphia (215) 871-8324

Det 752 Wilkes University, Wilkes-Barre (717) 408-4860

Puerto Rico

Det 755 University of Puerto Rico Piedras, San Juan (787) 767-1410

Det 755a University of Puerto Rico Mayaguez, Mayaguez (787) 832-4040 ext 3382

South Carolina

Det 765 The Citadel, Charleston(803) 953-5005

Det 770 Clemson University, Clemson(864) 656-3254

Det 772 Charleston Southern University, Charleston (803) 863-7148

Det 775 University of South Carolina, Columbia(803) 777-4135

SOUTH DAKOTA

Det 780 South Dakota State University, Brookings (605) 688-6106

TENNESSEE

Det 785 University of Memphis, Memphis (901) 678-2681

Det 790 Tennessee State University, Nashville (615) 963-5931

Det 800 University of Tennessee, Knoxville (423) 974-3041

TEXAS

Det 805 Texas A&M University, College Station (409) 845-7611

Det 810 Baylor University, Waco (817) 755-3513

Det 820 Texas Tech University, Lubbock (806) 742-2143

Det 825 University of Texas, Austin (512) 471-1776

Det 835 University of North Texas, Denton (940) 565-2074

Det 840 Southwest Texas State University, San Marcos (512) 245-2182

Det 842 University of Texas, San Antonio (210) 458-4624

Det 845 Texas Christian University, Fort Worth (817) 921-7461

Det 847 Angelo State University, San Angelo (915) 942-2036

UTAH

Det 855 Brigham Young University, Provo (801) 378-2671

Det 855a University of Utah, Salt Lake City (801) 581-6236

Det 860 Utah State University, Logan (801) 797-8723

VERMONT

Det 867 Norwich University, Northfield (802) 485-2460

VIRGINIA

Det 875 Virginia Tech, Blacksburg (540) 231-6404

Det 880 Virginia Military Institute, Lexington (540) 464-7354

Det 890 University of Virginia, Charlottesville (804) 924-6831

WASHINGTON

Det 895 Central Washington University, Ellensburg (509) 963-2314

Det 905 Washington State University, Pullman (509) 335-5598

Det 910 University of Washington, Seattle (206) 543-2360

WEST VIRGINIA

Det 915 West Virginia University, Morgantown (304) 293-5421

WISCONSIN

Det 925 University of Wisconsin, Madison (608) 262-3441

Det 925A Marquette University, Milwaukee (414) 288-5383

WYOMING

Det 940 University of Wyoming, Laramie (307) 766-2338

INDEX

4245